FRESHNESS FOR THE FAR JOURNEY

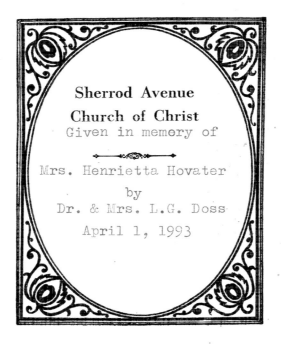

Sherrod Avenue
Church of Christ
Given in memory of

Mrs. Henrietta Hovater
by
Dr. & Mrs. L.G. Doss
April 1, 1993

FRESHNESS FOR THE FAR JOURNEY

Reflections on Preaching as We Step Toward the Twenty-First Century

Lynn Anderson

Foreword by Dr. Paul Faulkner

Edited by Lyn Rose

Freshness for the Far Journey

Unless noted otherwise, Scripture quotations are from The Holy
Bible, New International Version (NIV). Copyright 1973, 1978,
1984 International Bible Society. Used by permission of Zondervan
Bible Publishers.

Library of Congress Cataloging-in-Publication Data:

Anderson, Lynn. 1936 –
Freshness for the far journey/Lynn Anderson.
p.   cm.
ISBN 0-89112-153-6   92-70442
                                       CIP

Published by Abilene Christian University Press
Abilene, Texas 79699

Printed in the United States of America

To
J.C. Bailey,
Charles Coil, Sr.,
Wesley Jones,
Landon Saunders

*Each of these men
at his time, in his way,
left footprints on my soul,
and when I stand to preach
their voices echo through
the corridors of memory.*

CONTENTS

FOREWORD

For all of the years Lynn was at Highland, he was my kind of preacher. I am proud of his friendship and his work in the kingdom. He has blessed my life. He has stayed fresh and in touch with himself, his family, his church, and his God.

Lynn offers good, sound advice to those who are just starting out, but he offers more: an inspiring vision of the best that preaching can be and the great joy that touches the life of the man courageous enough to speak out for God.

Lynn is transparent and open about some of the pitfalls he has encountered in his years of experience, yet he is able to be optimistic, always looking beyond the difficulties to solutions. In my judgment, Lynn is at his best when he displays his rare ability to self-disclose with good taste. One never doubts his sincerity—the book rings with truth and honesty.

One thing that echoes throughout the book is his love of preaching. Lynn cares deeply, and he is able to articulate what events and actions have strengthened his love and his ability to stay on course in spite of all the satanic schemes that seek to pull a minister aside from his mission.

Dr. Paul Faulkner
Distinguished Professor of Marriage and Family
Abilene Christian University

INTRODUCTION

Few preachers from among Churches of Christ in the last half of this century have had as much influence on the state of preaching as has Lynn Anderson. He has inspired and encouraged two generations of preachers to preach boldly and biblically. He has exemplified preaching which is both passionate and pastoral, both challenging and comforting. Few preachers currently in their 20s, 30s, and 40s have not been influenced by Lynn, directly or indirectly.

During the late 1960s and early 1970s, preaching within Churches of Christ began to sound radically different than in previous eras. Rather than preaching topics laced with countless individual verses from the Bible, preachers began to center sermons around single passages in context and around entire books. Churches were being inspired (and changed) by Bible-centered sermons. For many of us who grew into adulthood during that time, the first expository sermons we ever heard were preached by Lynn Anderson. And they were exciting and enriching.

For me, Lynn has been model, mentor, and friend. And like dozens of other preachers, I have felt Lynn's personal interest and encouragement. Along with hundreds of my peers and associates, my life and ministry have been deeply affected by Lynn. And I am grateful to God for him!

This book in many ways represents a lifetime of work. While Lynn's specific preparation occurred over several months, the heart of this material he has developed—and lived!—over many years. He presented it to an appreciative audience of preachers and students during the 1991 Abilene Christian University Lectures on Preaching.

Tapes of those lectures have been listened to all over the world. Many have commented on how extremely practical the lectures were, not only in conceiving and constructing sermons, but, more importantly, in equipping the minister to be a person of character and godliness.

This book contains the heart of those lectures but is considerably expanded. The material is fresh, penetrating, and relevant.

My prayer is that you will be touched and encouraged by Lynn's message. More than that, I pray that this book will result in more effective preaching and more Christ-like preachers whose lives are given to God's kingdom and to His glory.

Dr. Jack R. Reese
Chairman,
Department of Graduate Bible and Ministry
Abilene Christian University

PROLOGUE

Jack Reese and the folks at Abilene Christian University graciously invited me to deliver the 1991 spring Lectures on Preaching. For this I was unspeakably honored. These lectures appeared to be well received and are finally ready to be published in a book. When I began writing, eighteen months ago, alone in the stillness of a Texas Hill-country ranch-house, I sat and stared at the glowing computer monitor, wondering if the words I would string together would really matter very much.

I suppose I *should* have something to say about preaching. After all, I've been at it for over thirty-five years, in churches of all sizes in several cultural settings. I spent nearly a decade of my life in academic preparation for the task, and another decade or more trying to help train others. For nearly twenty years a stimulating and thoughtful church provided study time and a broad forum which have continually challenged me to give my best efforts to preaching. Some of today's finest minds freely open their treasure-houses to me. Colleagues fuel me with affirmation and good will. And, yes, occasionally, some pilgrim will stumble out of this or that decade and thank me for some word that made a difference.

I *should* know what I am doing. But I realize at a very profound level, that I really don't. Preaching is in large part a gift. I do not know why some of my preaching appears to connect and change lives. Maybe some bright homiletical technician could dissect my efforts and explain them, but I certainly cannot. For me, *Mysterium Tremendum* shrouds the preaching enterprize. In fact each passing year only broadens the parameters of my ignorance about this astonishing thing God is doing in those who preach. It all enchants and mystifies me. If you want the truth on it, I'm not sure anyone understands it much. Oh, yes, there are ways we can help each other some, but after all the empirical research is tabulated, distributed, and implemented, the mystery of preaching still transcends our clumsy and often contradictory explanations.

Yet, when the invitation came, I eagerly agreed to do these lectures. I'm not completely sure why. Likely, at least in part, because my hungry ego would tolerate no alternative. How audacious it is for anyone to preach, let alone to try and tell others how. Much of my experience of the preaching mystery is too subjective to recommend and too personal to reveal.

However, in another very true sense I was compelled by a strange passion to verbalize some of my reflections on preaching. Besides I am deeply indebted to so many comrades at arms who have made the fruits of their labors freely available to me. If indeed I do have anything helpful to offer, I cannot but reciprocate with great joy.

What I have written in these pages, however, is not so much about preaching as it is about *being* a preacher. This is, to me, the central issue. Most of my colleagues seem to agree. In preparation for this assignment, I circulated a questionnaire to a number of them. The bottom line of their response was, "How do I stay spiritually and professionally alive in the midst of a hurried and overcommitted life?" Or, in the words of one preacher, "How do I keep all the plates spinning, yet stay fresh over the long haul?"

So, for the beloved circle of my fellow preachers and those others who do not preach yet but who are feeling heaven's tug toward the pulpit, I have assembled these thoughts with warm prayers that through God's enabling Spirit they might encourage you in the sweet agony of preaching.

Lynn Anderson
Dallas, Texas
February 1992

Section

1

WHO IN THE WORLD DO YOU THINK YOU ARE?

How can you believe if you accept praise from one another, yet make no effort to obtain the praise that comes from the only God?

John 5:44

Trust in the Lord with all your heart and lean not on your own understanding; in all your ways acknowledge him, and he will make your paths straight.

Prov. 3:5-6

1

CRISIS OF TRUST

My friend Don says that one of the occupational hazards of being a preacher is telling strangers what you do. You may find yourself on a plane or at a social gathering when the question is innocently dropped, "What do you do for a living?" Some may be tempted to lie, like Ray Stevens in his old country western song, and say, "I'm a logger." But most of us feel constrained to tell the truth. Then the fun starts, often at the expense of our self-esteem.

"Oh, my brother-in-law is a preacher." (His look tells you he doesn't think much of this brother-in-law either.)

He may apologize for his salty language or the joke you just laughed at uproariously.

Or he may be a member of the Full Gospel Businessmen's Association and proceed to give you his testimony. (This only happens if you're in the window seat of the plane.)

Each of us preachers has survived his share of such humorous moments. But laughter often betrays a deeper pain. The real issue here is not our ability to handle an awkward social situation with savoir-faire but our very selves as ministers. Our uneasiness betrays a lack of comfortableness in being who we are as men of God. The question does not ultimately revolve around our answer to a total stranger, but the answer within us which sustains our life and ministry.[1] When someone asks you what you do, he is really asking who you are.

Who Gave You the Right?

Who in the world do you think you are?

When Karl Barth faced the task of preaching, like many before him and since, he was overwhelmed by the audacity of it. He reflected:

> What can it mean? It means above all that we should feel a fundamental alarm. What are you doing, you man with the word of God upon your lips? Upon what grounds do you assume the role of mediator between heaven and earth? . . . Who dares to preach knowing what preaching is?[2]

Is there really any sane human being who stands to preach, confident that he is the man for such a job? What right does anyone have in the pulpit? Who is qualified to preach?

The question stands in even bolder relief against America's current "crisis of trust." Our times don't trust preachers much. Even most believers don't trust preachers. Yes, the crisis of trust stems partly from the recent televangelist debacles. But, most church folk don't really expect to find their preacher pilfering church funds or in the bed with a deacon's wife. The real crisis I speak of is not *that* variety of shattered trust. Rather, we are seeing a pervasive, quiet, almost subconscious distrust of those claiming to be pilots on the voyage of life and death, but who calmly scrub the decks while the cabins blaze.

People are subtly but deeply affected by this blasé attitude. Many thoughtful people simply don't take us preachers seriously. They have quit expecting their preacher to make a difference. Not, mind you, because they think no difference is needed, or that preaching cannot make a difference. They just don't expect *their* preacher to make that difference. As Eugene Peterson writes,

> No one seems to think we mean what we say. When we say "kingdom of God," no one gets apprehensive, as if we had just announced (which we thought we had) that a powerful army is poised on the border, ready to invade. When we say radical things like "Christ," "love," "believe," "peace," and "sin"—words that in other times and cultures excited martyrdoms—the sounds enter the stream of conversation with no more splash than baseball scores and grocery prices.[3]

People have seen too much plodding and pleasing and passivity. They half expect their preacher is too benign and too mundane; too protective of his security, his forum; too egocentric. In fact, a lot of preachers themselves don't seem to expect anything significant to come from their own ministry.

You Are the Message

Yes! Oh, yes! Ministry is suffering a crisis of trust far deeper than a few sensational sex and money scandals publicized by the media. Yet, a lot of the people that I know keep looking for preachers who not only speak for God, but who *are* the message. Because, of course, preaching is not mere communication, it is infinitely larger than that. And we communicate far more than what we say in our sermons.

A circle of ministers sat one afternoon awkwardly reflecting on our pulpit loneliness and confessing our sense of inadequacy. Eddie Sharp, minister of the large University Church in Abilene, Texas, sat in the circle with us. Eddie's father also sat silent in our circle, listening. "Sharp senior" has been a preacher all of his adult life and has two sons in ministry. A lot of people know him only as "Eddie's Dad." His whole ministry has been in small churches. Most of these churches he left better than he found them. Some he left sooner than he would have wished, usually with tears but never with bitterness. In our circle that day, Eddie sent warm tears rolling down his father's cheeks as Eddie recalled, "Here sits the man who has made the difference for me. I don't remember much about his sermons. I just remember what kind of man he was." Tears bathed my cheeks, too.

My wife, Carolyn, often mentions Elaine Burton, a Sunday school teacher in the little

Tupelo, Arkansas, country church when Carolyn was just a child. Elaine has surfaced in so many of our conversations that one day I asked Carolyn, "Tell me some of the things Elaine Burton taught you." Carolyn sat quietly awhile. I think I could see her eyes peering into the long ago. Finally she answered a bit wistfully, "Well, I don't actually remember any specific things she taught. I just remember *how she was!*"

That's it! Our listeners remember some things we say, but mostly they remember how we are. And the memory impacts how they are. It also determines how they hear what we say. So who do I think I am?

We Choose to Become

Of course, we are all of us sinners, deserving of death. That's who we are! This is not just a theological "truth"; it is a moral, ethical, and relational reality. And no one of us is any less infested with original sin than the next guy. Yet, in a real sense we are also who we choose to be. God allows us to *choose*, in spite of His Sovereignty. Allows? No, He *decrees* that we will become who we choose to become.

We must keep on choosing moment by moment, till the end. We will never have arrived. We will always be "becomers." God-ward choices however are not simple for anyone, especially in the environment of a fallen world that will not automatically facilitate and reward integrity. But preachers who want to rise above the crisis of trust require uncommon courage for the journey.

2

UNCOMMON VALOR

A group of respected brotherhood leaders sat on the platform at ACU as pugilistic preachers fired questions from both right and left. One brash cross-examiner rose and levelled a blast at the revered late Reuel Lemmons, "Has it not been historically validated, Brother Lemmons, that movements born to laud freedom and pursue truth usually crystalize into sectarianism, which ultimately turns on those who best pursue the movement's original aims?"

The questioner remained standing, assuming he had Lemmons on the defensive. But Reuel sauntered to the microphone, and in his dry Texas drawl, spoke only one word, which brought down the house.

"Yep!"

Make no mistake about it: Preserving internal freedom and integrity is not easy. Nevertheless, this freedom and integrity are indispensable in the development of healthy faith and thus to the maintenance of spiritual vitality. Jesus said, "How can you believe if you accept praise from one another, yet make no effort to obtain the praise that comes from the only God?" (John 5:44). Cowardice will definitely rob us of vitality. The preacher who surrenders to cultural or ecclesiastical environments which discourage freedom to pursue truth will stymie the growth of his own faith.

John Westerhoff in his book *Will Our Children Have Faith?* saw faith developing through stages.[4]

"Affiliative" Faith

After the "infancy" of faith, which he calls "experienced" faith, Westerhoff describes a more significant second stage as "affiliative" faith. In this "childhood" of faith (which doesn't necessarily coincide with biological childhood), one believes this or that because the group with which one is affiliated believes such things. Some teenager, for example, may spout "five steps in the plan of salvation" or articulate the "platform of the church," although he or she might scarcely be able to defend them. This is a normal and healthy part of faith development provided one does not get stuck there.

"Searching" Faith

Next is "searching" faith, a sort of "faith adolescence." When a child enters biological adolescence, compliance often melts away, and everything parental gets challenged. Wise parents know, however, that adolescence is a healthy developmental stage. In Westerhoff's analogy, adolescent faith (which can occur at any biological age) also questions and challenges. I believe the analogy is on target. Most thoughtful preachers will not only question, but downright disagree with their affiliative context at times. And the ecclesiastical "powers that be" often feel threatened by this: "Don't you love the church?" "Are you trying to cause trouble?" "Who fed you those lines?" Even politically-minded "friends" might back away from such searchers.

These forces conspiring to squelch exploration at this crucial stage of faith development have driven some questioning preachers toward negative options. For example, you know some who leave and go where questions are welcomed. You can likely think of others who can't muster the courage either to leave or to be openly honest, so they stay in the pulpits but seethe with unresolved anger, flailing about to the spiritual peril of themselves and everyone around them.

Then there is a third and I think much larger group of those who don't want to clash with friends, family, or tradition. They don't feel angry anymore, but they lack the courage to be honest about their questions. So they stay in their pulpits, swallow their questions, and refine the art of tuning out their own consciences. They simply capitulate at "affiliative" levels, go numb, and play out the mundane church game. This option is the most dangerous of all! The minister who chooses this path will eventually dismantle not only his own integrity but his very capacity to believe. "How can you believe if praise from one another is more important than the praise of God?" Although these ministers conform, something about them will no longer ring true, and they will further contribute to the crisis of trust.

"Owned" Faith

Westerhoff calls the next stage "owned" faith. By this time, "searching" faith has "found" some substance, and the person is "owning" his or her faith. He or she owns understanding of it and also owns the cost and consequences of it. This does not mean all questions are answered or that all views are correct. But it does mean that faith is now internalized, so that the believer can say, "On this I put down my life no matter where He takes me." Freshness, vitality, and resilience characterize this kind of faith.

However, here is the shocker: Some observers estimate that 70% of religious people, including church leaders, never move past "affiliative" faith. If that estimate is true, it means most preachers get stuck at "affiliative" faith! This is a sobering possibility.

A side note here for Restoration people: A clear and central difference between Denominationalism and Restorationism is precisely the difference between "affiliative" and "owned" faith. That is, a person may hold to "the full biblical truth" on doctrine (if any one person knows all that means) and still be Denominational, if his or her "views" are sourced in "affiliation" and not in the honest conviction which comes through openness to God and His truth. Whereas another person might yet hold to a number of unbiblical views and still be a "Restorationist" if his or her faith is "owned," being sourced in reverence for God and firm integrity which longs to pursue God's truth at all costs.

The Cost of Integrity

Our Restoration heritage has always praised the "noble Bereans" of Acts 17:11 because of their "owned" faith. The Bereans "examined the Scriptures every day to see if what Paul said was true." In fact, the apostle Paul himself would have remained a rigid, parochial rabbi till his death if he had lacked the courage to pursue truth beyond "affiliative" faith.

I have always admired the courage of my parents and the honest frontier environment which nurtured their freedom. The mercury had dipped to 32 degrees below zero that cold Canadian day in 1936, when hardy homesteaders lugged a cattle trough into our kitchen. They hauled water from the well, heated it on our coal-fed stove, and then filled the trough deeply enough to baptize Mom and Dad. My parents were laughed out of their social circles for a time, because they dared to leave the security of "affiliative" faith in order to pursue truth and embrace their "owned" faith as "Restorationists."

In moments of introspection, I am puzzled by my own attitudes: Why do I admire my parents' courage, yet get "antsy" when my children, in the tradition of their grandparents, sometimes "own" conclusions and values which don't match mine? Would I discourage my children away from the purity of heart which I have so much admired in my parents? Would I want my kids to stake a homestead and become permanent settlers on the theological territory my pilgrim parents saw only as a "frontier"?

Don't Shrink Back

Of course, I do cherish my understanding of the faith deeply enough that I want my children to have it, too. Yet, I pray that they will love God enough to pursue His truth as they understand it even if their search leads them in directions which break my heart. Fact is, pursuing truth will at times crush and break all of us! But, I implore you, my preaching friends, let us not shrink back from this pain.

Merle Crowell tells the story of a Greenland Eskimo who joined an American Arctic expedition.[5] For his faithful guide service he was later rewarded with a visit to New York City. His eyes were dazzled by the wonders, and he couldn't wait to describe what he saw to the folks back in Greenland. Upon his return he told of "stacks of igloos which reached almost to the clouds," and "other crowded igloos moving along the trail," and "lamps which burned without seal oil." But, the village people did not share his excitement over the new discoveries. Instead they gave him fish-eyed stares, tagged him "Sagdluk" (that is, "The Liar"), and shunned him. By the time of Sagdluk's death, his original name had long since been forgotten, and he carried the name "Liar" to his grave.

Later, Knud Rasmussen made his expedition to Alaska, guided by another Greenland Eskimo named Mitek. Mitek, too, was rewarded with a visit to the city, and although he was dazzled by the sights, Mitek remembered the fate of Sagdluk; to save his own reputation, he spun stories which his villagers could swallow. He and Rasmussen had "paddled a huge kayak on the wide river Hudson, through plentiful flocks of geese and large herds of seals." The villagers liked this story better. Thus, Mitek, who was actually the real liar, gained a place of permanent and extraordinary respect among his home villagers, while the man who had told the truth was called "Liar" and died in ignominy.

Face the Chill Wind

Should we be surprised that those hardy preachers who exercise the freedom to pursue truth often face such a chill wind? Remember Jeremiah, in the well? And Jesus, on the cross? And Stephen, stoned? Galileo? Luther? My parents, and possibly yours?

Some years back, at Abilene Christian University lectures, I helped facilitate formal discussion by a group of brotherhood opinion leaders on *The Worldly Church* by Richard Hughes and Leonard Allen. During the course of the lively exchange, someone asked, "Is it really possible for preachers to freely explore truth and pursue their honest convictions in our brotherhood?"

I answered that one of the reasons I remain in our fellowship is that here I find as much freedom to pursue my convictions as in any fellowship I know. After the session ended, I think I saw hurt in the eyes of two bright and compassionate young ministers who approached me and accused, "Lynn, you lied to us today. You, of all people, ought to know what happens to those in our fellowship who exercise freedom to pursue truth as they see it." While I think I understand what these brothers meant, I still insist we are free in our fellowship to pursue truth, but I didn't say we could do so without cost! There is no integrity without cost! Anywhere!

Freedom: A Condition of the Heart

We cannot expect to obtain freedom to pursue truth through some ecclesiastical fiat, nor will fallen humankind one day automatically rise up en masse to reward this freedom. Nonetheless, each of us is as free as all truth seekers have been from Jeremiah to Sagdluk, provided we, like they, value truth highly enough to maintain the payments. Such freedom does not come through legislation, nor by preserving some ideal religious movement. Rather, freedom is a condition of the heart. It is rooted in integrity and demands choices of the will. Jesus said, "If anyone *chooses* to do God's will . . . "(John 7:17, italics mine). We must choose to be *free* before God's will, no matter what the cost. This is a painful choice for the preacher. There is no denying that. But it is nonetheless absolutely essential to authentic ministry, even to authentic faith. As each Lord's day rolls around, no soul in the church house is in more spiritual jeopardy than the soul of the man in the pulpit.

As Oswald Sanders said,

No one need aspire to leadership in the work of God who is not prepared to pay a price greater than his contemporaries and colleagues are ready to pay. True leadership always exacts a heavy toll on the whole man. The more effective the leadership is the higher the price to be paid.[6]

Without such raw integrity, we preachers *may not even be real believers!* Remember, it was Jesus who said, "How can you believe if you accept praise from one another," but do not seek the praise that comes "from the only God?"

Those who most freely pursue God's truth do so in spite of the fact that the environment does not encourage them. To be able to stand before His smiling countenance means far more to them than their security or their forum or the affirmation of their fellows. They seem strangely hungry for "the praise that comes from the only God." "How can you believe" without such hunger? Without such integrity, how can ministry survive, much less rise above the crisis of trust and radiate freshness for the far journey?

3

THIEVES OF COURAGE

Wolfgang Amadeus Mozart died at the age of thirty-six. On a drizzly, cold morning he was buried in a pauper's grave. His wife did not even attend the funeral. There ended the agony of the man and began the glory of the artist.

Mozart had lived much of his life in mental torture. He floundered in moral and relational chaos. But in spite of major flaws in the man's character, at least one special virtue lay close to his soul. Part of the reason Mozart ended up in a pauper's grave was, according to legend, because he said, "I will not write what they want to buy. I will write what I hear." Such was Mozart's artistic integrity. Question: Can any preacher of the Word do less? Dare we neglect "what we hear" to live and preach only what "they will buy"?

How can I put the finger on my own private crisis in character? What specific thieves most often steal our courage? From the constellations of factors which conspire to soften our spines and buckle our knees, I identify here just three specifics which I constantly battle in my own heart. They also pop up regularly in conversations with other preachers who trust me enough to be transparent with me (or whose pain has become so intolerable that they are ready to throw caution to the wind, and spill their guts to anyone who will sit still and listen).

Soft Motives

First, soft motives often pilfer our courage. Each spring semester I begin teaching my ACU graduate course in ministry by asking the students why they want to be ministers. As they respond, we list the motives on the board.

Platitudinous Idealism

The list often begins with platitudinous idealism. They usually assume such "correct" answers are expected. This lasts only a few minutes, however, till some student sniffs out what is going on. Then the list becomes more honest, sometimes brutally so, even sliding to self-flagellation at the bottom of the list:

> • "I'm a natural speaker, and preaching
>   is a sure way to get an audience."
> • "I love to be front and center."

- "The 'position' is a cheap ticket to 'respect.'"
- "It's not too hard, and I'm basically lazy."
- "I like to be in control."
- "My parents groomed me for it, and everybody in our church expects it."

Then the discussion usually slows to a more reflective pace, revealing their fears about ministry.

- "There is little money or prestige in it."
- "There is little security and no retirement or perks."
- "I'm not sure I can make my mark in ministry."
- "All the preachers I know are nerds."
- "I don't like living in a fishbowl."
- "I love my freedom and don't want to live by role expectations."

Higher Motives

As the discussion unfolds, the mood usually shifts again, toward higher motives:

- "Doing something as important as the ministry will give me a sense of worth."
- "I think it will be very fulfilling to make a difference in the world."
- "I love people."
- "This seems to be where my gifts lie."

At first blush these motives seem noble and altruistic. But most classes contain a veteran or two who smile wryly at the idealism. From their own experience, they can recite volumes on shattered dreams, numbing discouragement, swamps of low self-esteem, wracking painful criticism and disappointments, balls of rage, and other inner destroyers which have dogged their ministries and long since exhausted the motivating energy of superficial "do-goodism."

So the list continues:

- "The world is in such a mess, and lost."
- "The great commission demands it."
- "I've got to be a soul-winner; God is pleased with nothing less."
- "The need is so great."

These motives are more substantial. But again, the veterans usually strip them back for what they are—guilt, religiosity, fear, desire to be significant.

Greed

My motives have run this gamut. I suspect that if you have been in ministry very long, so have yours. And the disheartening fact is that I keep recycling the list. My experience confirms Henri Nouwen's observation that much ministry is marked by anger and greed.[7] Greed? Yes, not necessarily greed for money, but for attention, respect, well-being, self-worth, or fulfillment. Sometimes it's greed to be doing something worthwhile, to receive spiritual blessing. Even, (get this) greed to go to heaven!

Anger

And the anger? Anger begins to build because nothing works. The people don't respond well, or they perform poorly or won't co-operate or appreciate. Sometimes the anger is aimed at the church or whoever it was that got us into this. At times the anger becomes self-directed at our own ineptness, or laziness, or ineffectiveness, or low motivation, or poor prayer life, or downright sinfulness, or some other ill-defined issue. We simply don't match up to our own expectations, and anger seethes.

Guilt

In not a few preachers, the anger eventually identifies God as the "culprit." He is the one who sucked you into this. He cooked up this whole system that doesn't work. He is the one who doesn't deliver according to my expectations. Here, guilt often joins anger in a toxic combination. "How can I let myself become so bitter toward people whom I am supposed to love? And, horror of horrors, will lightning strike me because I feel angry with Almighty God?" So greed and anger and guilt feed each other.

Heart of the Motive—God's Glory

What has happened? Usually, we have not worked the list far enough, not gone to the heart of the motive. The glory of God is the focus of life, and the nature of God the central motive for ministry. The Westminster Shorter Catechism is right on the mark when it states, "The chief end of man is to glorify God and enjoy Him forever." This is not true because it is in the catechism, rather someone put it in the catechism because it is true!

In Ephesians, the apostle Paul underscores God's glory as the motive of ministry: "He chose us in him before the creation of the world to be holy and blameless in his sight . . . that we might be *for the praise of his glory*" (Eph. 1:4, 12, italics mine). "In him we were also chosen . . . for the *praise of his glory*," and He sealed us with "a seal, the promised Holy Spirit . . . to the *praise of his glory*!" (Eph. 1:11-14, italics mine). "To him be the glory in the church and in Christ Jesus throughout all generations, for ever and ever! Amen" (Eph. 3:21). When our hearts look for this motive, our eyes can see it in nearly every chapter of the Bible.[8]

Looking back across the Old Testament, even the most dull eye cannot miss God's glory in the call of the ancient prophets. Glory dominates each scenario. For them, ministry was not a choice made from evaluation of human giftedness or longing for personal or religious fulfillment—not even refined altruism. Their ministry was to the glory of God!

Witness Isaiah, for example. "I saw the Lord seated on a throne, high and exalted." The flying seraphim shouted, "Holy, holy, holy is the Lord Almighty; the whole earth is full of his glory." In the midst of this earthshaking, soul-shattering encounter with the Almighty, Isaiah's personal aspirations came unravelled. Isaiah himself comprehended his own "unravelment," and sensed the "undoneness" all around him, in his world full of "unclean lips" (Isa. 6:1-5).

Only after God's purifying red-hot coal had touched our fallen friend, was Isaiah able to hear the call of God—only then was Isaiah able to respond. But his response was to God. Not to the clamor of human need, not to the inner longing to earn self-worth, but to the awesome glory of the Holy One. Both motive and the measure of ministry issue from the nature of God.

Ray Anderson stands on this bedrock truth when he declares "Ministry is to God on behalf of people, not to people on behalf of God."[9] Otherwise, contends Anderson, God's ministry often falls prey to pragmatism and utilitarianism and winds up being measured by "what works" and "what people think they need" rather than in terms of the will and the glory of God. Thus, when the glory of God is the measure of ministry, discouragement and disillusionment are less serious threats to the minister who feels very ordinary.

When God cut Isaiah's orders, they were not contingent on results through human responsiveness. In fact, He armed Isaiah with such a dangerous message that it would actually damage human hearts if they rejected it. Besides, God told Isaiah that the people would not listen. And to top it all off, when Isaiah asked how long before his ministry would get results, God said to stay and preach "until the houses are left deserted and the fields ruined and ravaged" (Isa. 6:11). From a purely human perspective, Isaiah's mission was to be an exercise in futility.

But at the very heart of Isaiah's motivation, God planted the ever active antidote to discouragement, bitterness, and disillusionment. For Isaiah, ministry was not primarily to man on behalf of

God, but to God, on behalf of man. God wanted Isaiah to be faithful, whether or not he was successful! And as long as Isaiah and I understand that God's glory is the *object* of ministry and the *motive* for ministry and the *measure* of ministry, there is never lasting cause for despair over my lack of accomplishments. Soft motives sap our nerve. Solid motives feed strong courage!

Divided Hearts

A second vampire which sucks away the life-blood of our integrity and thus of our courage is a divided heart. Even after we have nailed down our motives and our call, scarcely an hour will pass without some distraction, worthy or unworthy, waving banners to attract our affections. Some of these may appear innocent, but they are deadly enemies. They entice us eventually to look somewhere besides to God for the focus of life. The distraction may seem even "spiritually promising" at first, but don't be fooled. God is All: Jehovah Jirah provides, and we are blessed. Jehovah Rophe heals, and we feel whole. Jehovah Nissi conquers, and we experience victory. Jehovah M'kadesh sanctifies, and we feel clean. Jehovah Shalom blesses us with peace, and we feel secure. Blessings follow blessings when we depend on God for our courage.

Distortion

However, even the blessings of God can become addictive if they are distorted to become the focus of life. Very subtly, the blessing can become more precious to us than God who gave it. Kahlil Gibran understands this well, "The lust for comfort, that stealthy thing that enters the house a guest, and then becomes a host, and then a master."[10] And when the blessing becomes the object, we'll take short cuts to get it. Paradoxically, the more we become addicted to blessings, the further we distance ourselves from their real source. One day we may wind up going through the right motions and intoning the right incantations externally, yet we will be inwardly hollow, having lost touch with both the blessing and the source. People in our pews sense this hollowness, and it fuels the crisis of trust.

Idolatry

The God of blessing did not say, "use me to get your blessings." He said, "You shall have no other gods before me" (Exod. 20:3) and "If anyone would come after me, he must deny himself and take up his cross daily and follow me" (Luke 9:23). He did not even bribe us with promises of personal fulfillment if we do what is right. He just said, "I am the way: Follow Me!!" He even promised further that "everyone who wants to live a godly life . . . will be persecuted" (2 Tim. 3:12). In addition, when we stray, God Himself "disciplines us for our good, that we may share his holiness" (Heb. 12:10). However, our deluded selves may misread both the discipline and the persecution. It will seem to us that God's way works against our well-being. Then the short cuts to "blessing" may grow even more appealing. Ironically, knowing the ropes like we do, even though our hearts may go bad inside us, still on the outside we will be able to work the church system well; so well, in fact, that it will not only tolerate our sellout, but unwittingly support our idolatry.

Self-Delusion

Eventually we can even bamboozle ourselves (at least in the Golden Calf moments of religious euphoria) into thinking we are still on the upward way. Here again we may be dangerously close to dismantling our very capacity to believe. Don't forget, Jesus said, "How can you believe if you make no effort to obtain the praise that comes from the only God?" He could have said, "How can you feel good?" but He didn't. He could have said, "How can you go on?" but He didn't. He could have said, "How can you hide it from the people?" but He didn't. He could have said, "How can you succeed?" but He didn't. He said, "How can you believe?"

John Henry Jowett understood self-delusion:

> Whatever creates in me a sense of power tends to make me atheistic. How? When I become conscious of the possession of any power, I begin to think of myself as a cause rather than an effect. I can stir human hearts, I can move my fellow men. Recognizing myself as a power, I begin to think of myself as a creator, a cause; and ignoring all other causes, I lapse into an atheism which leaves out God.[11]

In this state, moral and ethical courage will play on rubbery legs if they have not already been benched, or kicked off the team all together. A divided heart "doth make cowards of us all."

Dimmed Hope

When I don't have the guts to walk straight, I had best begin asking, "What am I really about—knowing Christ or self-protectionism? The glory of God or my own personal well-being?" Jesus said, "No man can serve two masters" If we don't abandon one or the other, sooner or later we will disintegrate. The shell may go on looking just fine. We may continue to hold the respect of people, keep our forum, and cling to the security of our position. But the fire will have gone out, and we will further feed the crisis of trust. Thus at subtle but profound levels, rather than help, we will actually dim the hopes of people we face each Sunday. Elizabeth O'Conner aptly describes this state,

> In the churches we no longer hear God speak.
> It is the minister who addresses us, and he
> does not claim communion with God. He
> walks in more humble ways. There is no
> chance that he will succumb to the arrogance
> of those who claim to have been to the moun-
> taintop and to have seen a vision. The last
> clergyman who said this we tracked down in
> the night and killed. Now there is no voice
> reaching across dividing walls to disturb us in
> our prejudices, and when the Sunday service
> is over, we can return to our home and live
> safe. No one will recognize and point out
> that we have been with Jesus. No one will
> notice in us a style of life different from his
> neighbor's.[12]

Indeed, a divided heart can quickly slip off angle into integrity crisis which saps our courage and drains the vitality from our ministry.

Hidden Sin

Soft motives then lead frequently to divided hearts. And these two inevitably lead to a third interloper that saps our courage: Hidden Sin. Burton Coffman, a veteran minister, pointed this out in a very earthy way when he was in his seventies a decade ago. He heard me preach a sermon in which I suggested that faith is, at its taproot, a decision of the will. After the sermon Burton beelined to me and boomed, "Decision of the will. That's right, boy. It's also a moral decision."

I asked him to help me understand more of what he meant.

"Well," he explained, "we have a way of adjusting our theology to fit our morality. For example, you show me a preacher who is getting too sophisticated and broadminded for the Gospel, and I'll show you a preacher who may be shacked up with his secretary!"

Burton understood how hidden sin which is not dealt with, buckles the knees of courage. All varieties of hidden sin have that effect, not just the scarlet sin in Coffman's colorful quote.

"Nagging Flaws"

At first, my pet sin and yours will likely seem to be no big deal. Only a nagging flaw! We all have faults, right? At times it may even masquerade as a friend and may seem liberating and fulfilling. But sooner or later comes the downside. As one brother said, "My cute little yapping puppy became a fullgrown rabid Doberman Pinscher." Although King David's hidden sin may not be the same as yours or mine, still he discovered this principle in spades. I believe Psalm 38 was written somewhere between Uriah's death and Nathan's confrontation. The euphoria of new adultery had worn off. Possibly David had looked across many a breakfast table at Bathsheba's morning ordinariness. Doubtless he had stared into the darkness of many predawn hours, imagining the look on Uriah's face when Uriah realized that his friend David had done him in.

Most importantly, surely David had locked eyes with a broken-hearted, but offended Holy God. "O Lord, do not rebuke me in your anger or discipline me in your wrath. For your arrows have pierced me, and your hand has come down upon me" (Ps. 38:1-2). How can we face God's terrible holiness while we are nurturing a rebellion, whether the sin is scarlet or any other color of the rainbow? It makes no difference. Sin not dealt with, big or small, is an affront to God's holiness.

Psychosomatic Illness

Perhaps it was as he stood before the morning mirror after one of those sleepless nights that David first uttered the words, "Because of your wrath there is no health in my body; my bones have no soundness because of my sin . . . . My wounds fester and are loathsome because of my sinful folly" (Ps. 38:3, 5).

Not only do the knees of courage buckle, but the body shows psychosomatic illness. Sometimes illness is waived aside as "stress-related": "My back is filled with searing pain; there is no health in my body. . . . My heart pounds, my strength fails me; even the light has gone from my eyes" (Ps. 38:7, 10).

I will definitely not be seeking God's face, much less growing, while I am hiding sin! Even if I know how to free myself of hidden sin, I may not be able to muster the will. And in this state I will likely be either unwilling or afraid to be known by God or anyone else. This will distance me from people, driving my social life to the shallows.

Social Shallows

As David said, "My friends and companions avoid me because of my wounds; my neighbors stay far away" (Ps. 38:11). David, is it really they who stay away from you, or you who avoid them? Years ago and far away, a co-worker with whom I had felt very close subtly began moving toward more impersonal conversation and slowly distanced himself socially from me. I searched my soul wondering if I had offended him. Then he began avoiding group devotions, even subtly making light of the need our staff felt for such times. He explained that he was wired differently and "that emotional sort of thing" was not how he got his spiritual batteries charged. He even implied that some of us were imposing our needs on the rest of the group. Self-doubt wobbled me. Time revealed, however, that this brother had drifted into the grip of gross immorality. Of course he did not want to be close to his fellow ministers and open with them, much less approach closer to the gaze of the Holy One.

Face to Face

H. G. Wells told the story of a certain fictitious New England bishop who was revered for his sensitivity and wisdom. People freely told him their troubles and he would usually ask, "Have you prayed about it?" He had discovered that if that question was asked in just the right tone, it seemed to settle things a bit.

However, the bishop never prayed much himself. He felt no need of prayer. He had things all wrapped up in a tight package, until one day his life tumbled in. He found himself so overwhelmed that he decided to take his own advice and pray.

On Saturday evening he entered the cathedral, went to the front, knelt on the crimson rug, and folded his hands before the altar. He could not help but think how childlike he was. Then he began to pray, "Oh, God . . . ." Suddenly a voice, crisp and business-like boomed out from somewhere above him,

"Well, what is it?"

Next day as the worshippers came to the Sunday service, they found the bishop sprawled face down on the crimson carpet. When they turned him over they discovered he was dead. Lines of horror were still etched upon his face.

The story is on target. A lot of us who talk a great deal about God would be scared to death if we saw Him face to face. Yet, that is where we preachers are called to live, face to face with Him in all His terrifying Holiness. This posture is incompatible with hidden sin. But it is the secret of humility, of hope, and of freshness. Such openness lies at the heart of the Isaiah experience and the experience of all men of God. The only thing that may take more courage than "preaching what I hear," is to stare into the eyes of a Holy God whose Word penetrates my very soul! I cannot escape the force of that realization. But, to see God is to see myself more clearly and to walk with fresh vitality.

Believe me, I know! I, too, have cycled through spells when the veneer was thick and glossy on the outside, but in my heart I was terrified of God. Out of a sort of "psychological self-protection," at times I even allowed myself to not even believe in Him. I have traveled through tunnels of darkness, outwardly gregarious, but intimate and open with no one. Have you? The name of this sin is irrelevant. The impact our sin might have on our reputations is beside the point, too. The size of the sin is not as important as the size of the grip it has on us.

Bottom line: "Am I willing to deal with sin which is buckling the knees of my courage, distancing me from people, separating me from God, and resulting finally in stale and impotent pseudo-ministry?" Make no mistake about it: Hidden sin will always sap our courage. The only way back to courage is confession and repentance. Listen again to King David, our ancient fellow struggler:

> When I kept silent, my bones wasted away
> through my groaning all day long. For day
> and night your hand was heavy upon me . . . .
> Then I acknowledged my sin to you and did
> not cover up my iniquity. I said, "I will confess
> my transgressions to the Lord"—and you for-
> gave the guilt of my sin (Ps. 32:3-5).

Oh, the wonderful release and renewal available through genuine repentance, confession, and forgiveness. Lost courage regained. Fresh vitality restored! "Therefore let everyone who is godly pray to you while you may be found; surely when the mighty waters rise, they will not reach him"(Ps. 32:6). This is God's promise for the journey!

4

SETTING THE ALARM SYSTEM

Do I hear someone say, "Lynn, this is all quite interesting, even a bit convicting. But I already knew all that stuff. I preach too, you know. Point is, *how* do I maintain integrity? How do I feed courage?"

To be perfectly honest, I can tell you a lot more about how to lose internal integrity and courage than how to gain and protect them. I am far more experienced at that. But by long trial and error I am assembling a burglar alarm system against the robbers of courage. Without this system I will always be dangerous to myself and to everyone around me. The things I have discovered are not intended to be "answers." But because these simple discoveries mean so much to me and have given me strength, I offer three of them for whatever they are worth. (Three, huh? Once a preacher, always a preacher!)

Transparency

First is *transparency*. A preacher friend from another state vividly demonstrated the folly of nontransparency. This good, but insecure man, who found it very difficult to be honest about his own frailties, stood in the pulpit one Sunday and in a moment of false bravado asserted "no woman can tempt me!" A certain little lady sitting in the audience crossed her legs and swung her high heeled shoe back and forth on her toe thinking to herself, "Well, we'll just see about this!" Before many weeks had passed, she toppled that preacher from his perch and devastated his life and ministry. There was nothing wrong with his ideals. He was ambushed by not honestly accepting his own vulnerabilities.

My ineptness in so many areas of life forces me to live in a confessional and grace-dependent posture. And you are as capable of rottenness as I am. Scripture says so. So was Paul, and he never forgot it for a minute. His claim to be "chief of sinners" was neither hyperbole nor false modesty. His humble-sounding confession was not merely a communication strategy intended to help him leap the intimidation barrier so he could identify with us "lesser mortals." Rather, it was Paul's personal reality. And, be sure not to miss his verb tense: not "was," but "am." Present tense!

Of course, transparency gets top billing in most books, lectures, and conversations on preaching these days. After all, it is the "in" thing to tout "transparency," and who wants to be "out of it"? However, we hear openness and vulnerability being recommended nearly everywhere but being implemented nearly nowhere. We do see several smooth imitations. But for me they are easy to spot, because I have become past master at them myself.

However, please don't hear me suggesting that you should neurotically dump your guts at every conversation. Rather, we should demonstrate an attitude of openness before people, awareness of vulnerability, and dependency on our God and His grace. Furthermore I am not suggesting mere self down-talk. Self-bashing undercuts credibility, too. Such prattle often merely parades a false humility. I do not need to perennially badmouth one of God's sanctified ones, even if that person happens to be myself. But we must continually, openly, and honestly remind each other that we are kept sanctified only by the strong embrace of His amazing grace, and not by some strength of our own. The moment I do anything in order to appear better or stronger than I really am, no matter how small it may seem, I have begun a deadly deception and set myself up for bigger and more horrendous things to come.

One minister tells of driving up to the church at midnight to pop in and encourage the group practicing for a Christmas program. Since it was late and the lot was empty and he was in a hurry, he wheeled up into the fire lane, jumped out of the car and ran in. No big deal. After all, it was just for a moment and he was *The Minister*! Next day, one of his staff members informed him that a teenager spotted the car and had wondered out loud, "What jerk would block the fire lane outside a room full of people?"

The minister later apologized to the whole church for this presumption and recklessness, and he even asked them to keep holding him accountable. For him, that one fairly innocent act was actually an early warning that he presumed privileged status and felt impervious to wrongdoing and had taken the first self-deluding step in a direction which could ultimately be disastrous. By his open confession before the church he was practicing an honest awareness of his own vulnerability which also cleared the way for accountability.

Accountability

Along with the need for transparency, I am discovering the value of *accountability*. Warning: My being accountable to you is of absolutely no spiritual value to either one of us if you demand it of me. But it is of amazing value if I request it of you.

Some years back in a state distant from my home, I spoke on the need for accountability. Later a young man cornered me privately with an unusual request. He said that he was a "flasher." He had periodically flashed for a number of years, but so far he had not been caught. He convinced me that he genuinely wanted to stop his destructive and God-dishonoring behavior. He had tried every remedy, but nothing had worked. Then he made this strange request, "You have convinced me that I might be helped by making myself accountable to someone. Would you let me be accountable to you?"

I protested, "But I live in another part of the country, and I will rarely see you, and I don't even know you. Wouldn't it be better for you to be accountable to someone here?" But I could not persuade him to muster the courage to confess to someone in his home church. So I reluctantly agreed to exchange periodic phone calls with him. However, I didn't really expect much from such a flimsy arrangement.

The phone calls continued occasionally for over two years, and from the very first one he told me that not only had he stopped flashing, but I saw him recently and he said he has even lost the compulsion to flash. I believe he is telling me the truth, and also believe that he finally had the courage to be open with someone near him. There is something powerful in the anticipation of frank and loving questions. Of course, professional counselors use such contracts routinely as a therapeutic technique to treat problems ranging all across the emotional landscape.

One minister who demonstrates accountability is Bill Hybels of Chicago. While Bill leads one of America's most visible churches and is respected across the continent, he makes his life totally open and accountable to trusted elders and associates. Once at a retreat I asked Bill to give me some examples of what accountability means to him. Bill replied, "Why do you wear the kind of watch I see on your wrist?"

"Because my wife gave it to me for Christmas," I replied, "and why do wear the one on your wrist?"

Without hesitation he explained, "Because the people to whom I hold myself accountable felt it was the kind of watch that I could handle, and that flashes healthy signals to the people I pastor."

As I gasped my amazement, an elder who had accompanied Bill on the retreat added, "and on the plane out here, Bill actually pulled out his financial record book and asked me to go over the ways he is using his money, to see if I could spot any danger signals." I learned later that Bill even refuses to travel unless accompanied by a family member or a Christian brother, again to practice and model accountability.

"Neurotically scrupulous," did I hear you say? Maybe. But I don't think so. My spiritual maturity is not to be measured by the willpower I can muster while lying naked beside my strongest temptation. Quite the contrary. We demonstrate our spiritual maturity best when, fully aware of our most dangerous vulnerabilities, we carefully preplan our defense; when we make ourselves accountable to trusted fellow Christians who know us well enough to spot danger signals and who love us enough to look us in the eye and say so. Paul the apostle advised, "Put on the Lord Jesus Christ and leave no opportunity for the flesh to have its fling" (Rom. 13:14, Phillips). James wrote, "confess your sins to each other and pray for each other so that you may be healed" (James 5:16).

Those of us who served together for years on the Highland staff know each other well enough that we could pick up on the tell-tale flicker of an eyelash, and we love and trust each other enough to raise the probing questions. I could never have survived without these beloved staff colleagues, and several other confidants and friends in the Highland church and elsewhere.

When I moved to Dallas to spend a year writing, I felt naked and vulnerable out on my own, with no one to answer to. So one of the first things I did was to beg alongside me two circles of accountability; one is some fellow ministers, and another is a small circle of godly businessmen.

As I travel, when Carolyn or some brother or family member is not with me, I plan ahead to "check in" with Christian friends when I hit the permissive disconnectedness of whatever distant city. I have done this for years. I don't trust myself. You shouldn't trust yourself either!

Reflectiveness

To safeguard our integrity against our dangerous selves, besides transparency and accountability, I also would suggest *reflectiveness*, regular periods of quietness for the purpose of self-evaluation. Each person will need to find his or her own time, place and style of reflective quietness. We are not all wired up the same way. Yet, it seems incomprehensible to me that a person could even hope to survive spiritually, much less grow in his or her walk with God, without some form of regular quiet reflectiveness.

Yes, quiet reflectiveness is old hat. But it's astounding how few people who presume to be spiritual leaders and to speak for God have any regular and structured time alone before Him. And of those who do, many use their alone time simply to prepare material to present to others. This usually means no new personal growth, no

naked dialogue with God, no reflection and introspection, no praise and adoration, no openness to
the Holy Spirit, but rather the mere repackaging
of material yanked from the files or pilfered from
the books and tapes of others. Thoughtfully preparing materials for the needs of others is, of
course, a vital part of the ministry task. But it can
never, never replace personal prayer, reflection,
and praise—all three.

If I do not begin my day with prayer, reflection, and praise, God knows it immediately. I feel
the loss of vitality before lunch time. Family and
co-workers can sense it by the middle of the afternoon, and by nightfall "she's Katy bar the door."

Prayer

Prayer does not come natural for me. I have to
work at it. Since my mind wanders when I pray si-
lently, I have decided to pray out loud. I also frequently write my prayers. This exercise provides
me a daily "prayer agenda" which I can follow during what would otherwise be lost moments (traffic
lights, waiting rooms, etc.). It also helps me remember specifics I might otherwise forget. It also
forces me to write down, in black and white, specific sins I have committed, so that they stare
back at me from the page.

Reflection

Then comes reflection: First reflection on the
Word, then reflection on the heart. For me, reflection on the Word does not mean "strip-mining" the
Bible for sermon nuggets. Rather I read slowly
and re-read, savoring the essence of the passage,
letting it wash over me. The Holy Spirit gives me
strength and perceptiveness from this approach.

But besides reflection on the Word, I also need reflection on my own heart. Here again, my journal helps me a great deal. Writing down my reflections tends to make them specific and clear, corralling the wandering mind. Also, writing primes the prayer pump and moves my reflections off dead center.

The greatest value of my journal, however, is that I can periodically review the issues dominating my thoughts and gain perspective on the trends of my life. Sometimes I am actually surprised at the progress I have made. At other times I am thunderstruck at how long and how frequently I have been confessing the same sin or how deeply some resentment will have invaded my personality. This kind of inventory helps me more quickly spot not only the soft motives and divided loyalties, but the hidden sins that sap my courage and vitality. Journaling also helps me see where I have camped too long and nudges me along to fresh things.

I must hasten to add another caution: Too much self-analysis can be demoralizing. In attempts to be honest, I easily slip into compulsive spiritual navel-gazing, which can wind up being a most insidious mutation of self-centeredness. For this reason, let me point from here to the place of praise in our reflectiveness. Praise focuses beyond ourselves. In recent years I am discovering a growing appreciation of the power of pure personal praise. Consequently, I habitually both begin and end my prayer and reflective time with praise.

Praise

Praise may take many forms. Sometimes I repeat a psalm. Sometimes I simply reflect on the goodness of God and let "stream of consciousness" roll. More often however, some structured resource helps. For the last few months, for example, I worked my way through Jack Taylor's book *The Hallelujah Factor*.[13] Just before that, Eugene Peterson's book *Answering God* guided me in praying the Psalms. Sometimes my praise is internal and silent, but usually it is aloud and occasionally (dare I admit it?) with hands raised, shouting at the top of my lungs.

God deserves to be praised. "Glory [is] due his name" (Ps. 29:2). He has promised to "inhabit the praise" of his people (Ps. 22:3, KJV). Yet, praise is a scary word in our circles. Especially when we read in the Bible how they shouted and sang and clapped and raised their hands—and even danced! They went wild in biblical times. They wrote poetry. They sat in silence. They gave soliloquies. They spoke the story. They shouted with song. The word of God is full of praise from one end to the other.

Praise refines our spirits. It drives away despair. Remember the Psalmist said, "You have turned my wailing into dancing, Lord" (Ps. 30:11). It refines the conscience, strengthens the faith, and sensitizes the soul to the presence and majesty of God.

Praise purifies our hearts. It is almost impossible to keep looking regularly into the face of the Christ, praising God with our full beings and persist in hidden sin at the same time.

Praise softens the nose of the cynic. Praise gives strength for the journey. It emboldens our hearts and lifts our discouraged brother. And, praise makes glad the heart of God. Who can come away from genuine praise without being refreshed?

A Caution Light

Well, these are some of my "discoveries." However, I offer them somewhat reluctantly for two reasons: First, describing one's own devotional life can sound like boasting, in fact, can actually *be* boasting. Even as I write these words I am not sure I have dodged this hazard. Yet I ran the risk because to urge quiet reflection without putting flesh and skin on some specific examples easily results only in a fog of platitudes.

Years ago I ran across the following story which illustrates a second danger which is much more serious. Many African nationals revered the famous missionary David Livingstone almost as if he were a god. In fact some called him "the Jesus Man." Consequently, they mimicked nearly every aspect of his life. As Livingstone worked in the fields with the Africans, at regular intervals during the day he would drop his tools and run out into the seclusion of the tall grass, fall down on his knees, and pray. Then he would trot back to his work.

Livingstone followed this habit with such long, disciplined regularity that he actually wore paths into the grass. The Africans called these "prayer paths" and curiously explored them. At the end of each of Livingstone's paths they discovered two depressions in the earth which were left by the wear of Livingstone's praying knees. Since the Africans wanted to be like the Jesus man, they needed "prayer paths" too. But they took a shortcut. Instead of wearing their prayer paths and knee holes by long use, they simply marched into the grass with their machetes, clearing paths and gouging holes. Of course, their naive imitations did not bring them the spiritual resources which God was pouring into Livingstone. They had only aped externals.

Somehow I suspect a lot of us are too ready to latch onto a borrowed gimmick. So I offer this word of caution. I have listed some specific mechanics which help me. They may be of no use to you whatsoever. It would be disheartening to doggedly clone another person's mechanics and still not connect with God. But on the other hand, it would be disastrous should you decide that you can keep your heart and life pure and your vitality fresh without any form of regular disciplined prayer, praise, and reflection!

So What?

Let us return to our original question: Who then indeed is qualified to preach? We do not have the right to preach simply because "we are gifted along this line." Nor do our academic credentials or "on-the-job" training alone qualify us for this task. Reputation among our fellows certainly does not commend us in God's sight as vessels of the Word. Not even our loyalty or our accomplishments. Not even integrity of character. In fact, even pure hearts do not ordain us for the pulpit. After all, "The heart is deceitful above all things and beyond cure. Who can understand it?" (Jer. 17:9). No human heart is perfectly pure.

Actually, we are never *qualified* to preach, but we are only *allowed* this privilege by God's amazing grace! "Through God's mercy we have this ministry," said the Apostle. There is no room for pride in our ministry because, "we have this treasure in jars of clay to show that this all-surpassing power is from God and not from us" (2 Cor. 4:7). The refrain of my heart resonates with my older brother:

> I became a servant of this gospel by the gift of God's grace given me through the working of his power. Although I am less than the least of all God's people, this grace was given me: to preach . . . the unsearchable riches of Christ, and to make plain to everyone the administration of this mystery . . . (Eph. 3:7-9).

So I repeat. The surpassing *Mysterium Tremedum* of this sweet agony called preaching is that I, that we, with our unclean lips should actually be entrusted to stand amidst a people of unclean lips and speak to the awesome glory of God!

Endnotes for Section ❶

1. Don Crittendon, "On Being a Preacher" (Unpublished paper delivered at Abilene Christian University, Abilene, Texas, February 1988).

2. Karl Barth, *The Word of God and the Word of Man* (Gloucester, Mass.: Peter Smith, 1978), 125.

3. Eugene Peterson, *The Contemplative Pastor* (Dallas: Word, 1989), 39-40.

4. John Westerhoff, *Will Our Children Have Faith?* (New York: Seabury Press, 1976), 37.

5. As quoted by Earle Nightingale, "Keep an Open Mind," Insight Tape #74 (Chicago: Nightingale-Conant Corporation).

6. J. Oswald Sanders, *As a Word in Season*, trans. Ilse Lasch (Boston: Beacon Press, 1963).

7. Henri Nouwen, *The Way of the Heart* (New York: Baltimore Books, 1982), 11.

8. See Pss. 34:3; 63:3; 69:30; 86:12; John 8:54; 12:28; 21:19; Rom. 4:20; 11:36; 15:9; 16:27; 1 Cor. 10:31; Eph. 3:21; Heb. 13:21; 1 Pet. 2:12; 4:11; 5:10; 2 Pet. 3:18; Jude 25; Rev. 1:6; 4:11; 5:12-13; and many other passages.

9. Ray S. Anderson, *Theological Foundation for Ministry* (Grand Rapids: T. & T. Clark, Ltd., 1979), 8.

10. Kahil Gibran, as quoted in "Think on These Things," *Christianity Today*, 19 November 1990, 46.

11. John Henry Jowett, as quoted in A. J. Gossip, "The Preaching of the Cross," *Prokop'e Newsletter*, VI, 1 (January-February, 1989).

12. Elizabeth O'Conner, *Our Many Selves* (New York: Harper & Row, Publishers, 1971), 114.

13. Jack Taylor, *The Hallelujah Factor* (Nashville: Broadman Press, 1983).

Section

2

WHAT ON EARTH ARE WE DOING HERE?

Therefore, since through God's mercy we have this ministry, we do not lose heart. Rather, we have renounced secret and shameful ways; we do not use deception, nor do we distort the word of God. On the contrary, by setting forth the truth plainly we commend ourselves to every man's conscience in the sight of God . . . . For we do not preach ourselves, but Jesus Christ as Lord, and ourselves as your servants for Jesus' sake. For God, who said, "Let light shine out of darkness," made his light shine in our hearts to give us the light of the knowledge of the glory of God in the face of Christ.
2 Cor. 4:1-2, 5-6

5

IMAGING GOD

Sundays rarely look alike. But, most of mine
begin much the same way. I rise before dawn,
often after a fitful night of restless dreams or of
staring into the darkness reaching for that elusive
insight floating just beyond the circle of consciousness. Alone in the bright early kitchen, I sip my
coffee and crunch my cereal while going over the
notes. In the shower I praise and pray, but quietly, so I won't waken Carolyn. Somewhere between the towel and the necktie I sense the
adrenalin rise and the emotions awaken. In the
car, I usually sing at the top of my lungs all the
way to the church.

Down in the dark and echo-quiet sanctuary, once more God listens to me groan my petitions. I pace the empty aisles with my hands raised in adoration and shout for the sheer joy (or is it for sheer dread?) of the approaching hour. I rehearse the message in my mind. Faces rise in my imagination. Judy got her ring last Friday. There is where John sits. He seemed more reflective than usual last Sunday. It's a year since Lula died. Over there, Gretchen. Her husband lost his job last week. And over there . . .

Soon these people I love will be gathering here, coming out of a variety of motives, bearing constellations of hurt and hunger, ranging from eager readiness to steely resistance. I cannot keep from anticipating how people will look as they receive the message. Some will trust me, others won't. Whether they recognize it or not, all will share a desperate need to hear a word from God.

Some Sunday mornings I feel very much alone in that cavernous auditorium. But I know that I am never really alone. God has promised, "I will never leave you or forsake you." My old friend "Sunday Morning Adrenalin" is always there, too, disturbing the lower intestine!

Why Am I Here?

Well, three songs and a prayer, and we're up to bat again. What on earth am I trying to do? And why? We call this thing preaching. And for God's sake, that is why I am here. Or is it really for God's sake? What *are* we doing here?

Fred Craddock says:

Preaching is extremely difficult to talk about; the most complex and difficult subject I know.

. . . Sometimes I begin my classes by trying to get the students to understand how complex the matter of preaching is. I create this situation: A student leaves the classroom, goes into the Common, sees a fellow classmate and says, "Were you in systematics this morning?"

"No. What happened?"

"Well, the professor lectured as usual for about forty minutes and then suddenly, for the last ten minutes, *began to preach!*"

"Then I say to my students, 'What, in your understanding, was the nature of the shift?'" And they all begin to talk about it. Some of the students say the professor must have raised the volume of his voice.

Probably.

The professor laid aside the notes and started speaking extemporaneously.

Possibly.

The professor became more agitated. (laughter)

The professor became more interested in the subject. (much more laughter, with applause)

The professor became more personal.

The professor looked at us and wanted us to receive what was being said.

"Did you take more notes, or fewer notes?"

"Fewer notes."

"Well, did the quality of the material go up or down?"

"Well . . . maybe down a bit."

What really was the difference?

One student said, "The Holy Spirit took over."

Possibly.

It is evident at the end of the hour that all of
us in the room know what preaching is. . .
none of us knows what it is! Defining preaching is a very complex matter.[1]

What are we doing here? At the risk of sound-
ing stuffy, the first observation must be theological. For me, all ministry is to God and must begin
with God. "In the beginning God."

Imago Dei!

Both the motive and the measure of ministry
issue from the glory of God. Three times in one
paragraph the Apostle says that our purpose is
"that we might be for the praise of his glory"
(Eph. 1:6, 12, 14). But notice: reflecting God's
glory means also to reflect His methods. That is,
to give God glory, we do things in God's way.

"And God *said* . . . 'Let there be' . . . and there
was" (italics mine). Boom! Just like that! God
spoke and all things burst into being. In the beginning, God "created" by His word! Since His word
is back of all creative power, the irreducible
minimum or life source appears to be not matter,
energy, or DNA, but communication. **Word!** God
is also "sustaining all things by his powerful
word!" (Heb. 1:3). So, because God speaks, we
after His image and reflecting His glory must also
speak! *Speaking is Imago Dei.*

God's Voice

Thus God's prophets spoke. Then at the full-
ness of time, "God [who] spoke through the
prophets . . . has spoken to us by his Son"

(Heb. 1:1-2). In Jesus, "The Word became flesh" (John 1:14).

Next the early band of Jesus' followers said, "We cannot help speaking" (Acts 4:20). We must "Go, stand . . . and tell . . ." (Acts 5:20).

God's powerful word, all across history, even through Scripture, bears an auditory ring. Through his witnesses God continues to speak in our day. "Today, if you hear his voice, do not harden your hearts" (Heb. 3:8).

Sustaining Word

Notice, also, the Hebrew writer does not say "read words about His voice," but actually says "hear" His voice. As Haddon Robinson says,

A power comes through the word preached that even the written word cannot replace. To the New Testament writers, preaching stands as the event through which God works.[2]

Peter, for example, reminded his hearers that they were born again "of the living and enduring word of God" (1 Pet. 1:23). How? The good news "was *preached* to you" (1 Pet. 1:25, italics mine). Paul agrees that through the foolishness of *preaching* God saves believers (1 Cor. 1:21, italics mine). "Hold firmly to the word I *preached* to you" (1 Cor. 15:2, italics mine). Thus, God's ministry requires a messenger speaking through personal witness in face-to-face contact.

Creative Act

Preaching issues from the nature of God and is preserved by the design of God. It is indeed *Imago Dei*! And preaching is infinitely more comprehensive than mere communication. Preaching reflects God's creative act, thus is itself a creative act. Preaching orders ideas which shape experience. Like the primal creative word of God, the preached word also gives form to substance and life to matter. The preacher can actually expect the word he speaks for God to change the very form and essence of persons. As Beecher says, the preacher sees preaching as "the art of moving men to higher life, and nobler manhood."[3]

Also, like God, the preacher speaks a *sustaining* word. Good preaching is a word "of life," "bread from heaven," "milk," "meat," and "honey." Preaching issues from divine revelation, from God! Which, again, sets it off from all other forms of communication.

Also unlike other forms of communication, preaching issues from the essence of character. I cannot merely preach my way into the likeness of God's glory. Our times do not assign credibility to a speaker just because he wears a clerical title and stands in the spotlight. Many of the people who sit in front of me on Sundays typecast preachers as drugstore variety celebrities, rather than as servants.

Since God also "became flesh and made his dwelling among us" (John 1:14), preaching which reflects the nature of God involves a bond of loving relationship between preacher and people. Preaching will not cut through the pervasive cynicism of our times and be God-glorifying unless the preacher listens carefully to his people, lives genuinely with his people, and serves his way toward credibility.

6

DECODING THE BIBLE

In a legend floating around some years back, J. B. Phillips, the Bible translator, is said to have confessed, "When I lay my hands on the ancient sacred texts in order to translate them into modern English I feel tremors up my spine akin to those felt by an electrician rewiring an old house without the benefit of turning off the mains." Mr. Phillips, I think I know what you mean. Often when I open the Bible to "decode" the message through my Sunday sermon, I feel the same trembling awe.

I believe the whole Bible is the inspired and authoritative word of Almighty God, and I trust it to reliably convey all the vital themes of the God-humanity relationship. I would not have spent roughly twenty hours a week for thirty-five years studying the Bible, if I had not believed this. So when I stand in the pulpit, my heart's sincere desire is to faithfully exposit the Word of God. Yet, at the same time I am painfully aware that my understanding of the message of God will be imperfect, limited and shaped by my own dull insight.

Our Colored Glasses

My pulpit will be colored by my view of inspiration, my hermeneutic, and my theology. Since these three issues fundamentally impact our preaching, we will be well served to understand something of the biases and presuppositions we bring to the preaching task. Let me illustrate out of my own perspective. I was not reared in Bible belt America, so the underlying assumptions of my world view may not completely match the norm in Southern settings.

On the one hand, I reject the classical liberal view of inspiration, which leaves us "hunting and pecking" through the Bible to find kernels of inspiration among the husks of human speculation. Yet, I also have difficulty with the classic fundamentalist view which acknowledges no problems in the biblical text. At one period in my academic training, some professors taught the classical fundamentalist flat dictation view of Scripture and its supportive apologetic. Yet, the "explanations" of "alleged" textual problems sometimes seemed forced, often begging the question. I found myself at times defining faith as something like "the will to believe that which I knew wasn't so." While the fundamentalist view may serve well in the company of uncritical "true believers," exposure to culturally and intellectually heterogeneous environments has eroded its plausibility for me.

What Kind of Bible?

It now seems apparent to me that the pieces of literature which make up the Bible were not meant to be spliced together in a way which eliminates all problems in the text. The ancient writers affirm that God revealed His message to them, but this does not necessarily imply that God used those writers as mere stenographers to record every detail in some sort of universal and heavenly language. Honest investigation reveals many minor problems in Scripture. Given that the Bible was conveyed to us in human tongue, marked by human personality (2 Pet. 3:16), assembled by a variety of human minds and hands (See Acts 1:1ff), from many different centuries, and differing cultural backgrounds, addressing a variety of situations and needs, and then has endured the process of manuscript transmission over nineteen centuries, some discrepancies are to be expected.

God's Activity

I have come to believe that the full locus of God's activity in and through Scripture does not rest on the ancient authors *alone*. God's activity can also be seen in the means through which Scripture and the canon have since been formed, that God not only shaped Scripture, He also preserved it. And I believe that He is involved in our efforts to interpret and apply the Scripture as well. For this reason, I pray for God to help me with my preparation and with my preaching, believing that He will do so. And for me, this view drives toward the heart issues of Scripture. When faced by chill winds of informed, hostile criticism, this view is much more resilient than classic rigid fundamentalism and certainly supplies more substance than the classical liberal view.

Naturally, I acknowledge some problems with this view of inspiration. However, I thumbnail these brief thoughts on inspiration, not in an attempt to exhaust the subject, nor even to explore it. I leave it to the role of careful textual studies and exegesis to carry us through these problems.

Rather, the preceding paragraphs have been included here only to illustrate the need to examine our own presuppositions and to hint at some of mine. I do not intend this to be even a full description of my *own* assumptions, let alone a full and orderly discussion of the nature of inspiration. To more thoroughly examine your own view of the nature of Scripture, several helpful volumes are available.[4]

A Word About the H-Word

As much as I would like to dodge the "H-word," I must at least tip my hat to hermeneutics even though this subject is up for the "overkill of the decade" award in our fellowship. I find it impossible to separate my hermeneutic from the way I preach. As Princeton professor Thomas Long aptly observes,

> The preacher takes the text and puts it
> through the paces of a good exegetical process.

The grammar of the text is analyzed, word studies are conducted, the probable *Sitz im Leben* is established, and so on. The handle is turned, the wheels spin, the gears mesh, and in the end out pops a reasonably secure version of what the text meant in its historical context . . . .

Now, so what? The exegesis yielded the information that Paul responded in such and such a way to a question in Corinth about meat offered to idols, a question that would never in a million years occur to anyone in Kingsport, Tennessee, or Fresno, California. So what? The preacher is simply told that now the gap must be bridged from the history of the text to the urgency of the contemporary situation. It is presented as an obvious next step, a child's leap across a puddle, but the honest preacher knows that the distance between [the principle in the original setting and its application in current experience] yawns wide, and the leap seems difficult indeed.[5]

This leap is our hermeneutic. Every preacher is employing some sort of hermeneutic, even if he is not aware of it.

Three-Point Hermeneutic

A popular Urim and Thumim of biblical interpretation for the non-instrumental wing of the American Restoration Movement, at least over the past two or three decades, has been the following: The Bible teaches exclusively by Direct Command, Approved Apostolic Example, and by Necessary Inference. Certainly, the Bible teaches by command, example, and inference, but this is only part of the whole story. In fact, this three-point hermeneutic has never been universally accepted as the whole story of biblical interpretation in the Restoration movement, even for Alexander Campbell.

In fact, the late E. R. Harper, one of the more conservative and staunch debaters in the non-instrumental wing of the Restoration movement, saw more than a three-point hermeneutic. In his 1955 debate with Yater Tant, Harper contended that besides (1) direct precept, (2) approved example, and (3) necessary inference, the Bible also teaches by what he called "principles eternal."[6] Harper embraced the eternal love of God as a hermeneutic principle.

I find several limitations to the three-point hermeneutic *if taken by itself.* For example, "inferences" rarely seem as "necessary" to one person as they do to another. And obviously not all Apostolic examples are deemed binding (i.e., footwashing, head coverings, and holy kisses, to name a few). Even direct commands in Scripture are not all universal, some being very occasional (i.e., "forbid not to speak in tongues" and "gouge it out and throw it away").

Without a sound exegetical approach to Scripture, "command, example, and inference" becomes a process by which we force our own views on Scripture. We provide the setting for Scripture rather than permitting the text itself to form the setting or occasion for the message.

"Occasional" Scripture

However, I perceive the whole of Scripture to be occasional, not constitutional. By "occasional" I do not mean "casual," but that each book of the Bible was written in response to a given situation

and to address the specific issue of that
"occasion." The individual authors did not see
themselves writing sections or subsections of a
universal constitution. Each expected what he
wrote to be interpreted in the light of his intent
on that specific "occasion." The ancient writers
would likely be surprised to see some of their
specifically targeted words generalized to apply
uncritically in all settings and for all time.

"Constitutional" Scripture

By "constitutional," on the other hand, I mean
the view that each individual book of the Bible
was designed to interlock with other sections to
form one whole unified and systematic constitution and that each section is applicable universally and for all time. (Of course, to say that the
New Testament is not a constitution does not
deny that New Testament faith is "constituted" by
Scripture.) Therefore, since I do not accept the
constitutional view, but rather see the documents
of Scripture as "occasional," I am not comfortable
using the Bible as one would use a book of case
law. Words, phrases, or concepts from one book
cannot automatically be cross referenced as if
they will always mean the same in another book.

While I am not ready to totally discard the traditional hermeneutic, some additional reflections
seem useful to me as I attempt to interpret
Scripture. Of course, these reflections, like those
on inspiration, also are incomplete and flawed.
Such will always be the case with any applied
hermeneutic, since hermeneutic is not a science
based on unchangeable laws of the universe, but

merely an approach, an angle of entry shaped by one's world view.

An Applied Hermeneutic

True, in its purest sense, the never-changing task of hermeneutic is to (1) determine the meaning of the text, (2) draw the principle from this meaning, and (3) apply the principle to the analogous current situation. In this sense hermeneutic is not dynamic and changing. However, one's applied hermeneutic in the sense of the specific method which each person or generation employs to accomplish this interpretive task is to some degree dynamic and ever-renewed as worldviews shift, contexts change, and personal rhythms rise and fall. So we will never complete the task of constructing a watertight and once-for-all-times hermeneutic.

Michael Casey says that finding a "new" hermeneutic to replace the "old" is a

> search for the Holy Grail . . . . The message of God is eternal, while the methods of translating and communicating that message will change as the situations and problems humans encounter, change.[7]

Yet I want my principles of interpretation to be informed from within Scripture itself, as far as that is possible. And where a system of interpretation is externally imposed, it should be acknowledged for what it is: an externally imposed system.

Many books on hermeneutics are available.[8] Let me encourage you to explore the subject. Get in touch with your own presuppositions and work out your own set of guidelines for interpretation and application. Here are some of mine:

The "First Importance" Guideline

While everything in the Bible may be equally true, everything is definitely not equally important. Scripture itself declares that some issues tower over others and are "of first importance," as opposed to the "flat" view which sees all biblical data of equal significance. And Scripture is not vague on the big issues. They stand out like neon lights. Some examples: (1) The death, burial, resurrection, and appearance of Christ are clearly said to be "of first importance" (1 Cor. 15:1-5). (2) The preaching of the cross (1 Cor. 1:21-23; 2:1-6). (3) Love of God and fellow man (Mark 12:29-31; 1 Cor. 13:13).

Biblical material gathers significance and clarity as it clusters around such "first importance" declarations. Baptism, for example, draws its meaning from Jesus' death, burial, and resurrection (Rom. 6:1-11), as does the Lord's supper (1 Cor. 11), discipleship (Matt. 16:24-26), and servanthood (Mark 10:45). These are only some obvious examples of the "first importance" guideline.

The "Recurring Themes" Guideline

Second, recurring major themes run through the heart of God's revelation in a unity through both Testaments. Such themes as Suffering Servant, Justice, Love, Mercy, Holiness, Transcendence of God, Faithfulness of God, Covenant, etc., are major recurring themes lending shape to scriptural interpretation. Significant materials and concepts cluster around these.

The Guideline of "Congruity"

Third is the principle of congruity: specific statements of Scripture are most reliably understood in the light of *all* the rest of Scripture. For example, the congruity principle would mean that the single passages concerning the role of women might be best interpreted in congruity with the sweep of Scripture, including the Fall and its consequences, roles God has women playing in the Old Testament and the New, the distribution of spiritual gifts among *all* Christians (Rom. 12:1-8), Paul's own assertions of mutual submission (Eph. 5:21-25), and those equalities which are fully restored in the cross (Gal. 3:28). This approach gives us a more balanced understanding than does interpreting the whole of biblical material concerning women through the "Rosetta stone" of one or two passages like 1 Tim. 2 and 1 Cor. 14.

The Guideline of "Historical Perspective"

Fourth, historical perspective aids me in interpretation of Scripture by alerting me to my own locus in space (current local context) and time (the history of Christian thought). Some questions I ask myself as I pour over my open Bible are these: What presuppositions inform my view? What issue gave rise to my current hermeneutic? What streams of thought brought my fellowship to its current view? What changes have taken place since former hermeneutics were hammered out which might affect their current usefulness? And, not least of all, what is churning in my church or in my gut, right this minute, which will impact my application of this text?

Other Concerns

Fifth, of course, literary, linguistic, and contextual concerns which intertwine around classic exegesis are indispensable to sound interpretation of the text.

"Story Form"

A sixth reflection has taken on major significance for me in recent years: The Power of Story. A case for this perspective on hermeneutics is helpfully articulated in a paper by Michael Casey of Pepperdine University[9] and by Hauerwas and Jones in their book *The Why Narrative?*[10]

H. Richard Niebuhr, notes Casey, observed that biblical writers and speakers clearly used storytelling to communicate theological content. Both the Synoptic Gospels and Acts employ narrative style to reveal theological content concerning "things which are most surely believed" and "all" Jesus did and taught.[11] Peter, Stephen, and Paul all recited the great events of Christian and Israelite history in story form in order to communicate core theology. (See Acts 2:22-36; 7:2-53, etc., for examples.)

Some preachers regard stories as too flimsy and imprecise to carry propositional truth or commands. However, in Scripture, proposition and command are often "embedded within narrative" and the narrative not only reveals them but gives them "their sense of meaning."[12]

Story is not necessarily myth or fiction but "human history and biblical account as grounded in story." The story is not personal subjective narrative, but "the story of Christ and the early

Church," and is less susceptible to "individualistic whims than are approved examples and necessary inferences."[13]

However, Casey agrees with Michael Goldberg that the metaphor and the narrative must be specifically "paradigmatic stories" that "make a claim about and upon our existence" not just stories that "are merely entertaining or moralistic" or that "can be reduced to mere myth."[14] These stories must both claim to be true and to ring true, and can

> sustain and transform our existence now and in the future. Paradigmatic stories say to us, "This is what happened so far, and hence this is how you ought to go from here." In the Bible, the Exodus story and the story of Christ and the early church have this quality.[15]

Deuteronomy 6:20-25 presents exhibit "A": "When your children ask . . . you will say, 'we were . . . '" and so is launched a theologically-loaded narrative.

Let me echo a warning sounded from several quarters: Story form hermeneutic has been given far too much dominance in some current circles. It is not the only approach to biblical interpretation, not even a dominant approach. Taken alone, story form hermeneutic can leave us with a toothless text. But nonetheless, taken along with the rest of my reflections, the story approach presents several helpful features:

> • Exegeses of Scripture will continue to be a central task of the church.
>
> • Things precious to our heritage (such as the Cross, baptism, Lord's Supper, and priesthood of believers) will be

retained, but in the more compelling and personal form of "the old, old story" in which believers participate personally, currently, and experientially.

- Listening for central biblical metaphors develops discerning ears which can better select from secular metaphors only those which clearly convey sound, biblical meaning without bringing along baggage common in secular metaphors.

- Story lends identity to the believer giving him or her a sense of place in the stream of Divine purpose and among the community of faith.

- Story form also helps the believer to connect in personal ways with major, deeply relevant, theological themes which, in their transcendence, sometimes are left to float only in abstract and ethereal realms.

Admittedly my "quasi-hermeneutic" as outlined here lacks the scholar's precision and is incomplete and untidy. Most any novice could drive a truck through the gaps in it, and many questions are left dangling. But, in spite of this, I find it more helpful than the classic three-point Restoration hermeneutic, for several reasons:

- It does not promise final completeness covering all eventualities with a simple rule; therefore I find it more tenable.

- Through this approach I'm drawn toward the central issues of Scripture and seem less interested in peripheral and superficial debate.
- Thus, this approach is much less divisive than the historical approach.
- This perspective drives my faith-roots down into broader based, richer nuanced, and more spiritually nourishing resources of Scripture.

How does all this affect my preaching at a practical level? Let us move on to exposition.

Expositional Genre

For more than twenty-five years I have attempted expository preaching. In early stages, I worked from a flat and constitutional view of Scripture and thus tended to be not only atheological, but moralistic, legalistic, and disassociated from "crisis." Or, in other words, I was boring. However, my view of expository preaching is evolving through stages. These stages could well be flagged by key books influencing me during each of those various eras. My pathway started with Donald G. Miller's *The Way to Biblical Preaching*, which improved my definition of and methodology for expository preaching. Then came the impact of Leander Keck's book *The Bible in the Pulpit*. Keck steered me away from the shallows of verse by verse style and out into the deeps of Scripture. Later John Stott helped me bridge *Between Two Worlds*, the biblical world and the "now" world. By then I was ripe for Haddon Robinson's classic *Biblical Preaching*, and still later several works by

Fred Craddock. While these are, of course, only a few of the books from which I have profited, these volumes do each mark a fresh stage in the development of my preaching.[16] I expect such development will continue to unfold as long as God lets me preach.

However helpful, this literature has not impacted my preaching nearly so deeply as have my experiences. My career has shuttled me between American and Canadian cultures several times, including both rural and urban settings and among distinctly differing socio-economic groups. For more than a decade now, I have walked with one foot in a large demanding and pluralistic church and the other in the academic setting of ministry training. God has also led me through painful personal external struggles as I have attempted to learn how to live with my fellowship and internal struggles with my own sinful heart and my troubling theological questions. And, of course like all who attempt to preach, I have often felt stunned and cut deeply by reactions of some who perceive me or my message in ways far different from what my heart or my words intended. All of these experiences keep altering my approach to preaching.

What Difference Does All This Make?

Stay with me now for the final purpose of this theological background: By now, hopefully you clearly see some of my basic assumptions. First, that I hold a high view of the *nature* of Scripture, that Scripture is self-validating and that its message commends itself "to every man's conscience in the sight of God" (2 Cor. 4:2). So I rarely deal in biblical apologetic. The people I preach to need the impact, not the defense, of Scripture.

Second, I also hold a high view of the *authority* of Scripture, that Scripture is the inspired and authoritative living word of God. To visually and emphatically underscore this, I hold my Bible in my hand as I stand before the congregation week after week, and I urge each member of the congregation to hold one as well. My sermons themselves are designed to lead listeners to physically open their Bibles while I preach. And in the pulpit, I quote and read Scripture generously.

Because I view Scripture to be authority, expository preaching is my preferred preaching genre. But I define "expository" my own peculiar way. By expository, I simply mean that I want the text to control not only the message, but the form and genre of the sermon. As long as a sermon faithfully projects the meaning of even a small section of Scripture into relevant connection with current experience, I would describe this (whether it is done inductively, deductively, narratively, or sometimes even topically) as "exposition of Scripture."

Extended Series

However, I prefer expository preaching which works through whole books of the Bible in extended series. This approach appeals to me for a number of reasons:

(1) It helps me sleep better on Saturday nights. I don't need to wring my hands at the end of the week over what I'll preach come Sunday, because the text will already have chosen my topic well in advance. And long early reflection on the

text in context brings a sense of calm confidence and anticipation to my Saturday nights.

(2) Knowing my text and topic well ahead simplifies sermon preparation. In fact, my routine (outlined in chapter eleven) builds the sermon in a cumulative and natural way so that when delivery time comes around, most of the sermon has already prepared itself.

(3) I prefer extended series from one book because substantial life-changing input demands ample nuancing and gestation time. Singular focus over extended time drives the message deeper into the life of the church than one-shot, hit-and-run topical approaches can.

(4) The extended form of exposition also enlists the congregation as allies in exegesis. After all, last week they read chapter three with me, and next week they will read chapter five, so "inquiring minds" quickly spot any fancy footwork I might try in chapter four. This helps keep my exegesis honest.

(5) A preaching program which follows through a book of the text shoves me off my favorite soapboxes and brings more balance to my message. The text itself usually rotates through a wide range of issues, assuring a more nourishing theological diet over the long haul, with less of my distortion and speculation.

(6) This approach makes "reproof and rebuke" more palatable because when the text boldly confronts sin, the congregation knows that the Holy Spirit, not the preacher, has chosen the message of the day. Thus individuals are less likely to feel that the preacher has singled them out. They will have seen the subject coming in the text

weeks ahead of the day the preacher brings it to the pulpit.

(7) More significant change comes about through direct confrontation with the unfolding text than with humanly chosen topics because the message relies more on the power of God and less on the cleverness of the preacher.

(8) Possibly most important of all: Long systematic attention to an extended section of Scripture changes the preacher first, before it gets to the congregation. Across twenty plus years, I have personally experienced the deep and significant change that has gradually come about first in my own life and then in the nature of a church through sustained, systematic exposition of whole books of the Bible.

How This Affects My Preaching

Third, my view of Scripture as primarily occasional, rather than constitutional, impacts my preaching in several ways: (1) My preaching will not attempt to dust off an ancient blueprint. I do not view "restoration" as defense of a position, but as ongoing discovery, change, renewal, growth, refinement, and adjustment of understanding and of life. For me, the goal of "restoration" is to restore men and women into right relationship with God. The focus of expository preaching, for me, is the current application of God's Word not the reconstruction of ancient biblical scenarios. Consequently, I am hopeful that people who hear me preach over a long haul will open their Bibles in order to understand God and re-frame their present relationship with Him. Hopefully, they will come to expect that not all the "good Christians" and "healthy churches" lived in the first century. I want them to be even more interested in what God will be doing in their future, than what He has done in the past.

(2) The occasional view of Scripture also discourages me from using the Bible in the pulpit as if I were applying a system of theological case law or interpreting a constitution. I rarely preach sermons of polemic nature, or topically link together lists of scattered verses. Thus, hopefully when my listeners' hearts are touched, they will be responding more to God and less to the rhetoric of the preacher.

(3) This aforementioned view of Scripture also steers me away from attempts to fit each book or letter neatly into an overall system of interlocking propositional truth as if each writer were drafting a section of a systematic theology textbook. Rather I attempt to let each biblical writer speak for himself, for his intended purpose. Hopefully, people conditioned to this use of Scripture will subconsciously begin listening for the living voice of God rather than merely "quoting a key proof text."

(4) Since story form colors my hermeneutic, I tend toward narrative styles aimed at altering attitudes and experiences rather than at merely transmitting information. I want my listeners to develop the habit of sensing the "biblical story line." Love of story also lures me into generous use of anecdotes not always merely as illustration, but as vehicles through which to convey propositional or abstract content. Besides, story is an effective tool for dismantling resistance.

Also, I have come to believe that sermons are often loaded with more freight than preaching can carry. Yes! Christians need systematic instruction in doctrinal, theological, and ethical content. Scripture clearly says so (2 Tim. 4:1-4, etc.). But, this demands long intellectual rigor, and the best place for such is not likely the Sunday morning sermon.

(5) Since I believe the locus of God's activity to be spread across the whole process of the formation, preservation, interpretation, and application of Scripture, I hold that "the preaching of the word of God *is* the word of God." Of course, this is not a claim to modern day revelation, but I do very much acknowledge the work of the Holy Spirit as He helps "reveal afresh" the meaning and relevance of the Word in each preaching event.

All of these observations imply that for me, preaching occupies a position of centrality and dominance in the total task of ministry. I commit the bulk of my work week to Bible study and sermon preparation. I long to see inspiration at work again next Sunday morning, not just in the first century.

(6) Since I hold a high view of the church, I want my preaching to be utterances in the midst of my "community of faith." The Word springs to life and power in the crucible of daily life. I want the church to experience a sense of bondedness and intimacy with each other and with the preacher. At its best, this intimate bond between preacher and church is so real that sometimes when speaking away from home I feel as if I am making love to a stranger (or, should I say, as I

would *imagine* this might feel). Guest appearances and taped sermons heard by those outside one's local church will register radically reduced impact, compared to preaching at home.

(7) Finally, as previously stated, high Christology makes Jesus and His cross the lens through which all of Scripture and all of life are viewed.[17]

My preaching will necessarily be colored by my theological perspectives, past experiences, and current situation; but in the midst of those, I must be committed first and foremost to communicating as clearly and uncompromisingly as I am able, the inspired and authoritative word of God.

7

CLOSING THE CIRCUIT

My electrician gave me my favorite metaphor for preaching. As I step to the pulpit, with one hand I grip the hot wire of the divine Word; with the other I touch the ground wire of human need, and in the act of preaching I "close the circuit." High voltage surges through me. In that event, I am on the cross.

"Hot Wire" of Sufficient God

The hot wire of the Word produces excruciating pain in anyone who genuinely connects with it. First comes the pain of laborious exegesis as is underscored in the past few pages.

But, beyond exegesis comes the infinitely sharper pain of confrontation with the living Word which disturbingly challenges beliefs, values, and conscience. Sometimes the Word calls me to believe and say some things which could be threatening to my security and to my forum. (Yes! The word of God may even jeopardize our very livelihoods.)

While preparing a series on David some time back, I found the Psalms drawing me like a moth to the flames of the terrible and transcendent holiness of God. I loaded some books, tapes, and a tent in my old car, and I looped a two-week round trip to Canada to visit my father, with David and the Psalms as my traveling companions. Solitude on the road and in the tent turned out to be anything but thrilling. It was terrifying. In the dark tent, undistracted and alone with my conscience, I seemed attacked by platoons of "demons" threatening to do me in. But the "demons" played minor league compared to the hardball from heaven! His word is "sharper than a two-edged sword" and struck deftly and painfully at my heart exposing my sins and laying bare my secrets. This was terrifying. I felt embarrassed, convicted, threatened, and undone as God peered into my very soul. This was not a first, however; I have experienced similar agony many times. Nor will it likely be the last.

My interfacing with the Word is most powerful and yet most painful during those moments when I find myself staring pointblank into the face of Almighty God! In the preaching process, I am both impaled upon God's sword and electrified with His high voltage. God's word connects directly with my life. Only then does He release me with a clear and compelling word of hope for others.

"Ground Wire" of Needy Humanity

The preacher must, however, engage more than the text. If he only knows the Bible, he doesn't really know the Bible. He must also know his people! Along with Fred Craddock, I do not hold a gnostic view of "preaching mystery." Real people sit in front of me as I preach. Craddock says,

> If a person is a good pastor, he does an exegesis of the congregation as well as of the text. He can close his eyes and tell you where the people sit on Sunday morning. Even a mediocre sermon to people who love you is great.[18]

To exegete the church, I cannot cling to the quiet safety of my study. I must go out and interface with my people hands-on, through bonafide relationships. I must do real acts of service for specific persons. This is what God did while in flesh among us. But in so doing, I sometimes find myself overwhelmed by the intensity of the hurt and confusion around me, indeed within me. These all-consuming demands of the human dilemma drain the strength from me. Besides, I am part of the mess!

Oh, yes, there is incredible joy in preaching. But, good preaching also brings pain. If Jesus is any example, this is the only way true ministry gets done. Long-term, life-changing ministry necessarily brings pain. When we invest ourselves in the pain of others, of course we ourselves will get hurt. In this way too preaching is *Imago Dei*. God didn't just risk Himself to suffer. He planned to suffer, and in His suffering on the cross, He communicated most compellingly. When we are called to preach, we are called to "share his suffering" (Phil. 3:10).

"Closing the Circuit"

Finally, as he turns to face the sea of up-turned countenances, the preacher closes the circuit. Again the preacher himself will fall under the force of the word from God. The naked passion of closing the circuit between the awesome surge of God's message and the crushing demand of human need will be even further life-draining, the surge of high voltage only more agonizing.

In the process of being a "closer of the circuit," the preacher goes to the cross week after week on behalf of mankind. He completes "what is still lacking in regard to Christ's afflictions" (Col. 1:24). The heart of preaching is grief work. The preacher actually embraces the grief of the world and the grief of God in redemptive circuit closing.

Ecstatic Agony

It is not easy for me to be consistent with my own theology of preaching. I must constantly re-dig my footings. In the ecstatic agony of the task I am constrained to keep asking myself,

- What theological core is this sermon implying?
- Is this message fair with the text?

- What view of Scripture prompts me to preach this message in this way?
- What signals about the nature of the Bible will this send to the congregation?
- What are these people needing this week?
- Will they meet Jesus today, or only get nice advice?
- How much are my own psychological needs clouding the message?
- Is this message prompted by the Spirit and bathed in prayer?

I don't plan to ever stop asking these and a lot of other questions.

A preacher who heads down the road into preaching marked by exegetical thoroughness, personal transparency, and bold integrity should be prepared for some loneliness and opposition. Such preaching is not always popular with entrepreneurial personalities who "manage by objective" and want immediate results, nor will it satisfy the legalistic mindset of those who like clear parameters and who order things neatly packaged. He will also be letting himself in for a lot of hard work; but given the long haul (discussed more fully in section five), I know from over twenty years of firsthand experience in expository preaching that such an approach will connect meaningfully with human experience at its deepest levels. I believe it will also be truer to the text of Holy Scripture. It will keep the preacher fresh for the far journey. Most of all, this approach to preaching will offer appropriate honor and glory to God.

Endnotes for Section ❷

1. Fred Craddock, from Hickman Lectures at Duke Divinity School, on *Preaching Today Tape Series #88*, produced by Christianity Today and Leadership, 465 Gundersen Drive, Carol Stream, Illinois 60188.

2. Haddon Robinson, *Biblical Preaching* (Grand Rapids: Baker Book House, 1980), 17.

3. As quoted in A. J. Gossip, "The Preaching of the Cross."

4. Helpful books on the nature of Scripture: Paul J. Achtemeier, *The Inspiration of Scripture: Problems and Proposal* (Philadelphia: The Westminster Press, 1980). James Barr, *Holy Scripture: Holy Canon, Authority, Criticism* (Oxford: Clarendon Press, 1983). James Barr, *The Scope and Authority of the Bible* (Philadelphia: Westminster, 1980). F. F. Bruce, *The New Testament Documents: Are They Reliable?* 6th ed. (Donner's Grove, Ill.: Intervarsity Press, 1983). G. B. Caird, *The Language and Imagery of the Bible* (Philadelphia: Westminster, 1980). Avery Dulles, "Scripture: Recent Protestant and Catholic Views," *Theology Today* 37 (April 1980): 7-26. Norman L. Geisler, ed., *Inerrancy* (Grand Rapids: Zondervan, 1980). Leander E. Keck, *The Bible in the Pulpit* (Nashville: Abingdon, 1978). Bruce M. Metzger, *The Text of the New Testament: Its Transmission, Corruption, and Restoration.* 2nd ed. (Oxford: Clarendon Press, 1968). Bruce M. Metzger, *The Canon of the New Testament: Its Origin, Development, and Significance* (Oxford: Clarendon Press, 1987). Roger R. Nicole and J. Ramsey Michaels, eds. *Inerrancy and Common Sense* (Grand Rapids: Baker, 1980). J. I. Packer, *Beyond the Battle for the Bible* (Westchester, Ill.: Cornerstone, 1980). Clark H. Pinnock, *A Defense of Biblical Infallibility* (Philadelphia: Presbyterian and Reformed Pubishing Co., 1967). Clark H. Pinnock, *The Scripture Principle* (New York: Harper & Row, 1984).

5. Thomas G. Long, "The Use of Scripture in Contemporary Preaching," *Interpretation* (October 1990), 344.

6. *Harper-Tant Debate*, Abilene, Texas, November 27-30, 1955 (Abilene, Tex.: Chronicle Publishing Company, Inc., 1956), 4. Also, E. R. Harper, *Harper's Charts Used in Lufkin Debate on "Church Cooperation."*

7. Michael Casey, "Scripture as Narrative and the Church as Storyform Community: A Proposal for a New Restoration Hermeneutic" (Malibu, Calif.: Pepperdine University), 24.

8. Helpful books on hermeneutics: Gordon D. Fee, *New Testament Exegesis* (Philadelphia: Westminster Press, 1983). Gordon D. Fee and Douglas Stuart, *How to Read the Bible for All It's Worth* (Grand Rapids: Zondervan, 1982). E. D. Hirsch, Jr., *Validity in Interpretation* (New Haven, Conn.: Yale University Press, 1967).

James D. Smart, *The Strange Silence of the Bible in the Church* (Philadelphia: Westminster Press, 1970). Anthony C. Thiselton, *The Two Horizons: New Testament Hermeneutics and Philosophical Description* (Grand Rapids: William B. Eerdmans, 1980).

9. Ibid.

10. Stanley Hauerwas and L. Gregory Jones, eds., *The Why Narrative? Readings in Narrative Theology* (Grand Rapids: Eerdmans Publishing, 1989).

11. Casey, quoting H. Richard Niebuhr, *The Meaning of Revelation* (New York: The MacMillan Company, 1962), 44-46.

12. Casey, "Scripture," 24.

13. Ibid.

14. Ibid.

15. Ibid., p. 23.

16. Donald G. Miller, *The Way to Biblical Preaching* (Nashville: Abingdon, 1957). Leander Keck, *The Bible in the Pulpit* (Nashville: Abingdon, 1978). John Stott, *Between Two Worlds* (Grand Rapids: Eerdmans Publishing, 1982). Haddon Robinson, *Biblical Preaching* (Grand Rapids: Baker Book House, 1980). Fred Craddock, *As One Without Authority* (Nashville: Abingdon Press, 1987). Fred Craddock, *Preaching* (Nashville: Abingdon Press, 1986).

17. Leonard Allen, *The Cruciform Church* (Abilene, Tex.: Abilene Christian University Press, 1989), 133.

18. Fred Craddock, *Preaching* (Nashville: Abingdon Press, 1986), 60.

SECTION
❸

HOW CAN I STAY UP WHEN THEY'RE GRINDING ME DOWN?

We rejoice in the hope of the glory of God. Not only so, but we also rejoice in our sufferings, because we know that suffering produces perseverance; perseverance, character; and character, hope. And hope does not disappoint us, because God has poured out his love into our hearts by the Holy Spirit, whom he has given us.

Rom. 5:2-5

8

THE ELUSIVE THING CALLED FRESHNESS

The place smelled like power. We sat in his corporate offices high above mere mortals plodding city streets below. He listened attentively to my "insights" on the future of the Dallas Cowboys, probably waiting for the conversation to shift, then he nailed me with this less-than-innocent question, "What makes you preacher types tick? You are dealing in the most valuable commodity in the universe. How come some of you grow stale? If you guys really believe what you are saying, why do so many give up or burn out?"

My friend didn't lean in for an answer. He was not hunting for information, but pressing me to examine my heart? It worked too. Why indeed? How would you answer him?

What is the difference between the "shrinkers" who plod on or burn out, and the "growers" who not only hang in, but stay fresh?

Not just businessmen ask preachers this question. Preachers ask it of themselves! The most common question that surfaced among my colleagues in preparation for this book was, "How do I keep all the plates spinning, yet stay fresh over the long haul?"

- You take time away from your own family to help someone, and he complains because you didn't come sooner and do more.

- You go the extra ten miles to meet somebody's needs, and you never get one word of thanks.

- You are on call twenty-four hours a day and often devote your mythical "day off" to conducting a funeral or a wedding, and people ask if you are busy.

- You use a part of your vacation for study, and people wonder if you are working hard enough.

- And there is always the specter of the beloved former minister or the successful neighboring minister

("What a great and godly man!")
haunting every assembly and every
elders' meeting.

Is It Really Worth It All?

Small wonder that you ask at times, "Is it
really worth it all?"

If you feel this way, you are not alone. A lot of
ministers I know live with chronic weariness
which pushes them toward the brink of burnout. I
share "the wearies" with you. At times I have
imagined that the source of my weariness lay in
factors beyond my control, the relentless demands
of people or the unreachable standards of God. I
was convinced that I could do nothing about the
forces at work against my endurance, hope, and
creativity. Feelings of failure, envy, and anger
dogged my days. Across the years, however, I have
concluded that these feelings are fairly wide-
spread occupational hazards for preachers, so I
have decided that I had better expect them and
learn to live with them. As Phillips Brooks re-
minds us, growth in ministry means "higher
heights of joy and deeper depths of sorrow,"[1] so
our only escape from the pain is to stop growing!

What does grind us down? And can anything
be done about it?

Confessions of a Plate-Spinner

In the first place, most of us eventually accu-
mulate entirely too many plates. Then to keep the
expanding plate collection spinning, we are forced
to step up the pace. The accelerating pace con-
sumes even more energy and leaves even less
time. Yet, paradoxically, without study, reflection,

and renewal which require time, we distance ourselves ever further from the only lasting source of energy and freshness. This vicious downward spiral gathers its own momentum, and it is grinding down a lot of us.

Thus, overloaded and underpowered, we experience too many failures and too few successes. We may be tempted to compare our own dull plodding with the bouncing gallop of the guy across town. So to our feelings of weariness, futility, and guilt we add the energy drain of jealously and resentment.

Somewhere in all this we may begin to lose our sense of purpose. By that time, we are really in the soup. For at the bottom line, as William Willimon says, "burnout in ministry actually results not from a loss of energy, but from a *loss of meaning.*" [2]

Again, trust me. I know. This is familiar territory to me. In my thirty-five years of ministry (nineteen of them in one church), I have passed through several cycles of staleness. During the low cycles, I have traveled at least two self-defeating trails. Sometimes, in attempts to revive feelings of purpose and vitality, I have tended to plunge into even further overcommitment and more frenetic activity. This only ratcheted stress up higher. Or, at other times I have settled into weary spells of stoic plodding, where "tomorrow and tomorrow and tomorrow creeps in its petty pace from day to day." In both moods I tend to neglect reflection time, thus drifting further out of touch with God, with others, and with my own heart. Oh, yes. I've been there!

How do we get from there back to freshness?

The Cutting Edge

First, let's make sure we know what we mean by freshness. I get cornered every now and then by someone wanting to know how to stay fresh. Sometimes we suspect he or she means, "How do I stay on the cutting edge, up on all the latest books, stats, demographic profiles, church growth techniques, illustration sources, tape 'phenoms,' on ad infinitum?" While all of these things might be helpful ministry tools, they are neither sources nor indicators of freshness. Taken alone they present only the illusion of vitality.

The God-hungry people who approach your pulpit each Sunday want you to be "in touch with the times" all right. But what they want a lot more is a preacher who is in touch with God and is drawing freely from the deep wells. They want a word from someone who has obviously been with Jesus. They don't need pollyannas. They want ministers who face the chill winds of reality, yet are not overcome by them. They long for soul-deep resources which are "new every morning." So do I. So do you.

In fact, the preacher who expends his best energies presenting himself as "the resource person on the cutting edge" will almost certainly drift toward the shallows, not only in his message, but in his own soul. He will not have time to drink deeply of the waters of life. He will become "an empty cistern that holds no water." And in so doing will be an unwitting co-conspirator in the crisis of trust and character.

The Smiling Face

Freshness does not necessarily wear an effervescent smile, either. In fact, vitality sometimes comes dressed in sack-cloth and ashes, covered with blood and scars, bathed with tears. Sometimes freshness is very weary, even depressed. One does not need to be "up" all the time in order to be refreshingly on target, to emanate joy, or to stir hope.

Some of us are emotional pushovers. I'm one. For me to pretend otherwise would be as phony as an undertaker trying to look sad at a thirty thousand dollar funeral. Consequently one of my most difficult challenges is handling mood swings, and I still have a lot to learn about separating emotional cycles from the realities of spiritual well-being. Occasionally I pass through long arid periods of semi-depression longing to experience some religiosity. At those times I moan with David, "How long, oh Lord, how long," but I usually keep plodding on across these wastelands wondering if I will ever again feel anything deeply enough to weep over or to shout about. I have often associated these low emotional cycles in one-to-one ratio with spiritual failure and distance from God. In actual fact, they often result from fatigue, low blood sugar, a lousy sermon, a nagging critic—or prostate infection!

When I break through to a season of euphoria, physical vitality, emotional vibrancy, and positive thinking, I tend to assume this is when God is nearest, and that I am most certainly running the spiritual fast track. The only blemish on these glorious times is fear of losing them. I often find myself clinging to the highs, dreading

the lows, and contriving pump-up techniques.
Again in actual fact, these highs may realistically
not be "seasons of refreshing from the presence of
the Lord" at all, but may result merely from a few
good nights' rest, some regular exercise, a sermon
that "worked," a couple of affirming letters—and
some antibiotic for the prostate! So the long look
has helped me put these mood swings in perspective and to identify them for what they usually
are—mood swings, and usually nothing more.
They come and go, sometimes with predictable
rhythm and at other times with surprising sud-
denness; they are quite normal and usually temporary. So sometimes the way to deal with the
"lows" is simply to preach, pray, and plug away.

I am coming to trust that while my emotions
flap like a flag in a gale, God doesn't move. He is
the same, yesterday, today, and forever. He promised, "I will never leave you or forsake you." He
may be doing the biggest work in us when we feel
the lowest. The mountain peaks are fun, but the
thin soil on the summit is not nearly so nourishing of spiritual fruit as that rich dark stuff in the
valleys.

Freshness Is . . .

To be fresh then must mean something more
than being either the guy with the latest idea or
the one with broadest grin. Rather freshness is
ringing true, being on target. To be fresh is to
make sense in the deep places, to keep growing,
to evidence a current walk with a living Christ, to
radiate hope.   Freshness brings with it a breath
of life.

One day I walked into the study of the late and legendary E. W. McMillan, then nearly ninety years of age. He looked up from his papers, smiled warmly, and waved me to a seat. "Hold on just a moment," he said without dropping his pen, "I don't want to lose this thought." In a few moments, he closed his book, rose, and shook my hand vigorously, booming, "I never noticed that before. I am going to be a better man and a better preacher because of what I learned this morning." Then he added, "for all these years, I have tried to learn at least one new thing about my Lord every day." "Brother Mac" well personifies what freshness for the far journey means to me. I can say, "Me, too, Brother Mac." God knows that if I don't learn at least one new thing about my Lord every day, both my people and I are soon in deep weeds.

Several years later, John C. Stevens, Chancellor of Abilene Christian University, sat by McMillan's wheelchair and interviewed him publicly. Even though the old saint's mind wandered into the fog at times, at other moments his comments nailed the bull's eye of contemporary experience, and the freshness of his spirit transcended his failing body and antiquated vocabulary. He had seen it all. Time had ground him down, but he stayed up. "Brother Mac" remained fresh for the far journey.

9

NOW REALLY, WHAT MAKES ME TICK?

Re-Examining Our Motives

Let us go back to square one. Burnout begins with bad choices, but, most of these wrong choices may be traced back ultimately to things gone wrong at the nerve center. Somewhere along the way we may have settled for motives which are too meager and a call which is too small to sustain our sense of purpose and meaning.

Remember from chapter three: The primary *motive* for ministry must be the glory of God. If not, the *measure* of ministry often becomes merely religious human accomplishment, which in turn often degenerates into ministry fueled by anger and greed.

So a giant step toward vitality in ministry is fearless inventory of motives. No human being is entirely without mixed motives, but we must be honest about them and continually identify the shoddy ones for what they are and root them out.

Self Inventory

First, and at a very practical level, we can take some of this inventory ourselves, with pencil and pad in hand. Simply identify and list specific motivations, noting the soft spots. Ask yourself brutally honest questions like:

- What drives me?
- What is my balance between teaching and serving?
- Why do I hurry from the pulpit to the accolades in the foyer?
- How much am I in love with the head table, the attention of "pulpit groupies," or the feeling of doing something significant?
- Why do I linger for praise and run from criticism? etc.

You know how to draft your own list of questions. But physically write down your inventory.

Friends' Inventory

Second, for further help in assessing my heart, I also turn to the circle of trusted friends to whom I have made myself accountable. I ask them to shoot straight and help me spot danger signals. If you don't have such a circle, the fact that you don't may be a danger signal in itself; that you really don't want your life to be an open book. Run, don't walk to the nearest phone and begin assembling such a circle!

Professional Inventory

Third, if you fear that your heart may be seriously confused or deluded, ask a trained professional to walk you through a systematic personality inventory. This has been helpful to me and many others. In fact, let me carry this even one step further: At times I have become so entrapped in my self-constructed house of smoke and mirrors, that I have difficulty separating honest emotions and true beliefs from fabrications created for effect. Have you felt this way? If so, some clinical time with a competent counselor or therapist can help untangle convoluted emotions from issues of the heart. You may benefit greatly by this. I know because I have. Seeking professional counseling does not spell shame or failure. Rather this choice may express wisdom and integrity for someone who really wants to be God's person.

The Right Stuff

The central issue is this: "What really makes me tick?" "Whose glory do I indeed seek?" and "Who honestly is my Lord?"

One subtly misguided form of "servant-heartedness" believes that the demands of all the church people must be served. Thus the church becomes our Lord. But Paul didn't see it that way. He said, "men ought to regard us as servants of Christ" (1 Cor. 4:1). The servant word here is *huperetas*, or "under-rowers," a metaphor drawn from the slaves chained to the oars in the ship's belly. Orders from the captain and no one else marked out the rhythm of the oarsmen's strokes. Imagine what confusion and frustration would result if the galley slaves attempted to take their orders from the cacophony of tourists' voices on the deck? The oars would become hopelessly tangled, and the boat would fall behind the rest of the convoy. Stress would mount. The oarsmen would be demoralized, out of touch with the captain's wishes and envious of the crews who were passing them up. We are servants of Christ! He alone calls the signals and sets the pace.

Paul drives home his point in 1 Cor. 4:4-5,

> My conscience is clear . . . . It is the Lord who judges me . . . . He will bring to light what is hidden in darkness and will expose the motives of men's hearts. At that time each will receive his praise from God.

Who is the master? Christ!

We serve people best when our hearts long most deeply for the glory of God. When our activities flow out of the will of Jesus rather than from our own need to maintain favor with the whole church, we will also find our own work less stressful and more productive.

10

PAINTING THE BULL'S EYE

Viktor Frankl in his book *Man's Search for Meaning* maintained that no force outside ourselves can ultimately hijack our naked human freedom. "The last of human freedoms," he declared, "is the freedom to choose one's attitude, regardless of the circumstances."[3] Here lies one key secret to freshness for the far journey. We are not victims. We can make choices.

But instead sometimes we make excuses. Some of us become whiners, dreaming about this and wishing for that, all the while complaining about the array of forces conspiring to shackle us.

Our language betrays us. "I can't," "They won't," "I wish, but," "It won't work," "If only," etc. These are victim words. More accurate words might be, "I have or have not chosen," "I am, or have, or will," etc. Choice is the key difference between the *whiners* and the *winners*. Ultimately you choose the specific "plates" you are going to be held accountable to "keep spinning." So re-examining our motives, then, leads naturally into the next step toward freshness for the long haul: clarifying our mission.

Clarifying Our Mission

When I was on the Highland Church staff, David Wray and I frequently found ourselves sitting before frustrated ministers, attempting to encourage them. I recall one brother who felt overwhelmed with the "weight of the church hanging around his neck." He felt put upon by too many expectations. He enjoyed little cooperation from his church, and he lacked confidence because of what he saw as his inadequate ministry training. We gently suggested that he might want to re-enter graduate school to upgrade his skills, but he said he didn't know what the courses were and besides he couldn't afford them. When we suggested he check a catalogue and talk with the financial aid people, he complained that he didn't have a catalogue and besides he didn't feel comfortable talking with them, since he was not part of their tight circle. When we suggested that he might take the initiative and introduce himself to the circle and that they would be eager to receive and help him, he only dodged the suggestions, returning to his litany of congregational woes.

Although he would not face it, like many of us disheartened ministers, his basic dilemma resulted from his choices (or lack thereof). He will never get his life on target until he paints a bull's eye.

He is not alone. I have visited with many who share this paralysis and sometimes find myself hampered by it too.

Choose

The first step out of the victim mentality is "choose!" One of the more helpful human resources I have stumbled onto lately is the work of Stephen Covey in *The Seven Habits of Highly Effective People.* Covey helps me single out the specific "plates" I most want to "keep spinning," and to gradually and gently stack the others on the shelf. The first basic habit Covey observes in effective people is that they take charge of their own lives, or as he says, "Be Proactive."[4] Here again we confront the pivotal power of choice, that one ultimately manageable variable in human destiny. The Bible frequently underscores this principle: "Choose for yourselves this day whom you will serve" (Josh. 24:15), "How long will you waver between two opinions?" (1 Kgs. 18:21), "If anyone chooses to do God's will, he will find out whether my teaching comes from God" (John 7:17).

Spinning the Right Plates

Covey would say that I must choose to "begin with the end in mind,"[5] that is, clarify my life's mission. He even suggests a simple technique: Write eulogies from several people important to you that you would want them to deliver at your funeral. These eulogies will tell you a lot about what you want your life to count for. This exercise has been very liberating for me, helping me more clearly see what plates I want to keep spinning. I will keep those which are moving me in the direction of my purpose. Most of the rest, the ones that keep me running in circles, can gradually be retired.

This retiring may take you some time, because your calendar will doubtless be cluttered months ahead with things you have allowed to be imposed by extraneous demands which do not contribute to your mission. Your habits will be cluttered too. But given time, both calendar and habits can gradually be taken over by purposeful and productive activity: by things you intentionally choose, because they help get you where you want to go. Interestingly, once we know our objective we will not only know what to *do* but we will also see more clearly the things we will *not do* any longer.

Time to Decide

Carolyn and I loved the local ministry and the Highland church. Those people became "our family" across nearly twenty years together. Yet another dream, another sense of call, kept rising up in our path. For some years we felt a growing desire: (1) to help churches mobilize to reach a lost world which matters to God; (2) to work for spiritual renewal and for change in our fellowship toward congregational formats and strategies which can better connect with our culture; (3) to encourage leadership styles which implement such change; and (4) to encourage and enable the planting of new and more culturally appropriate congregations in North America. We had dreamed of cutting loose from other ministry for a year or two to follow these objectives through writing, (We wanted to write down the best things we had to offer our fellowship, thus giving these things broader circulation and longer impact.), seminars, and preaching. Many circumstances, plus the longing of our hearts, led us to feel called to this ministry. So Carolyn and I felt the time coming when we would need to bid the Highland family farewell.

But after all the years at Highland, leaving seemed almost like betrayal of the relationships we had developed. Besides, how would we support ourselves if we should cut loose to write? We have little retirement laid up, and soon I will be beyond the "marketable age" for many of our churches. Would it not be foolish to give up our security at this point in our lives? And after thirty-five years of effort that have resulted in a sizeable forum among our people, should we risk it all on a dream?

Carolyn and I both believe that part of God's guidance comes through the feelings and insights of our mates. The combined intuitions of two people are bound to be more accurate than those of just one. I would interpret strong negative or positive feelings from Carolyn as part of God's leading. She would feel the same way about mine. We believe that no minister should expect wholehearted support from his mate in a ministry chosen without the mate's full participation in the decision-making process. So Carolyn and I dialogued these dreams for over half a decade.

The dreams and the call would not go away. In fact they grew more vividly compelling as time went on. Then came that special ordinary day in the spring of 1990 at Hickory Ridge, Arkansas, where Carolyn's mother lives. I was preaching in an old time revival. Mornings found me running down the gravel roads, with the Arkansas green and the stillness of the country morning washing my soul. Every step of the run, I was turning over and over in my mind our dream and its cost. I knew at profound levels that the only things holding us back were reluctance to leave the fond relationships, the financial security of the Highland church, and the related forum such a visible pulpit provided.

Suddenly the decision broke out of its ethereal and murky cloud cover. It became very clear to me that no one else would tell us when the time had come to follow our dreams. In a burst of self-realization, I saw myself at eighty, sitting in a rest home, angry at myself for lacking the courage to follow our dreams and our call. Somehow, I knew that I had no choice left. But how would Carolyn react? Covering the return miles in record time, I burst in the door and announced, "Honey. We're going to do it. I am going home to resign the Highland pulpit." Carolyn's thoughts had been moving along the same trajectory. Her response? "Good! I think the time has come!" Once the decision was made, then, our next steps became crystal clear.

Specific Mission

I am convinced that few ministers have any specific life mission, any clear-cut, longterm objective. Some think they have a purpose statement, but it often is some catchall like, "preach the Word" or "help the church grow" or "win the lost," but with no specifics as to who, how, what, and when. This means they will not choose tasks and time use intentionally. Consequently they automatically find themselves consumed by crisis management, dashing between "spinning plates," while life wanders (or rushes) in circles. No wonder so many of us feel futility and sagging self-esteem, which lead to burnout.

You might say, "I know my purpose. Preaching is my focus." Of course, preaching will obviously be the central track of your mission or this book would not be for you. But what kind of preaching? For whom? For what?

New Frontiers

Frederick Jackson Turner, nineteenth-century historian, believed that the power which drives an expanding culture like America is its pioneering spirit which is always stretching toward a new frontier. The first frontier was the Atlantic, then the New World, then the West, and on to California. Without a new frontier, a culture begins to decay. What is America's next frontier? Space? Then what? Turner's insight applies to individual persons too. So, my preaching brother, what is your new and ever-expanding frontier? Where are you going? What is God's design for your life?

Once you know your ultimate objectives, then you can more confidently negotiate with a congregation what you can be expected to do and what you cannot be expected to do. This will best be expressed in a carefully written job description, formulated in dialogue with your elders or other church leaders. Your job description must take into consideration both your own life mission and the purpose statement of the church. But, once you make clear what you can be expected to do, then you can tack your weekly schedule to your office door, and your church will more nearly respect it because they will perceive your use of time to be purposeful. This will also help dispel that nagging guilty sensation felt by so many preachers, that "no matter what I am doing, I should be doing something else."

You cannot, however, make demands on a church. It may become apparent that the needs and dreams of the congregation may be incompatible with yours. (This does not mean theirs are wrong for them, or that yours are wrong for you.) But if such is the case, you may do an injustice to that church by trying to force it to conform to your dreams. If a mutually acceptable synthesis of your goals and those of the church cannot be reached, you might be well advised to plan a graceful, loving, positive exit—not to escape your circumstances, but to follow your life objectives and to allow the church to follow its chosen direction. If you do not follow your call, both you and the church will suffer in the long run. Mark it down: If you neglect your dream and your call in favor of your personal security, your heart will surely begin to die.

Warning! What I have just described cannot be accomplished by dashing off a Monday afternoon purpose statement. The process of setting your mission may take two to three years of reflection and refining. And, in actual fact, your life plan will remain open for continual midcourse correction as long as you live. However, you can be sure that if you do not know where you are going, like an airborne jetliner with no flight plan, you are sentenced to move in frustrating circles until you run out of gas.

11

REFINING OUR METHODS

Work Smarter Not Harder

God's nature and glory supply both the motive for ministry and the measure of a ministry's success. If you are examining your motives and clarifying your mission then you will also want to carefully select and continually refine the methods of your ministry. That is, actual ministry strategies must also reflect God's glory.

My preaching friend, God has called you to a ministry of the Word, prayer, and spiritual formation (equipping for ministry), not to be the church's professional plate spinner. As Eugene Peterson says,

> American pastors are abandoning their posts, left and right, and at an alarming rate. They are not leaving their churches and getting other jobs. Congregations still pay their salaries. Their names remain on the church stationery and they continue to appear in pulpits on Sundays. But they are abandoning their posts, their calling. They have gone whoring after other gods. What they do with their time under the guise of pastoral ministry hasn't the remotest connection with what the churches' pastors have done for most of twenty centuries.
>
> Three pastoral acts are so basic, so critical, that they determine the shape of everything else. The acts are praying, reading Scripture, and giving spiritual direction. . . . [yet] . . . It is possible to do pastoral work to the satisfaction of the people who judge our competence and pay our salaries, without being either diligent or skilled in them.[6]

Let me now become specific and practical. I have stayed in ministry thirty-five years (again, almost twenty years in one church). Sure there were some periods of regression and numbing blandness. But I feel more alive each year and feel fresher in my ministry now than ever in my life. This is a wonderful gift of God's grace! And God has taught me that to survive I must work smarter, not just harder. By trial and error along the way and with input from wise shepherds and mentors, God has given me some specific work habits which contribute to vitality. Again, they may or may not fit you. But here they are for what they are worth.

Promises

One, *make few promises,* but make the important ones and then put everything you have into
keeping them with excellence and joy. In Jesus'
parable of the two sons, one made lavish promises
but did not keep them. The other promised little,
but delivered well. This son, maintained Jesus,
did what his father wanted (Matt. 21:28-32).
Limiting the promises may take courage at first,
because some people will scream bloody murder
when you don't do what they expected. But in the
long haul you will strengthen your credibility.
Even a relatively short string of consistent deliver-
ies builds far more trust than a long list of shaky
promises. Of course you will find this practice to
be easier if you know your mission clearly. This
practice will also simplify your life and greatly
elevate your potential for freshness and joy.

Problem People

Two, *invest at least as much time in possibility
people as you do in problem people.* Obviously, life
powered by the love and compassion of Christ
dodges no problem people. They seem to have
caught the eye of Jesus, so they had better get
significant portions of our compassion as well.
Besides, some problem people have the potential
to become possibility people. But allowing ourselves to be consumed only with problem people
drains our energies, and in the long haul, actually
narrows the scope our ministry otherwise could
have had.

In the early stages of one of our church plant-
ings in Canada, Carolyn and I found our energies
consumed by very troubled people. A new mission

work often attracts the unstable fringe of the community first. I shall never forget the weary moment of insight as Carolyn and I were driving home from yet another marathon "emotional first-aid" session. We turned to each other and both asked simultaneously, "Do we know any sane people?"

Problem people not only consume a minister's time and energies, but they can give him a warped and jaded perspective on reality. He can become overwhelmed with feelings of frustration and hopelessness. So, we must intentionally choose to focus significant portions of ministry on possibility people. They lift our spirits and give us positive, hopeful perspectives.

Also because they can mature and take on responsibility quickly, possibility people can be delegated part of the mission and equipped to do it much sooner than problem people. Thus, the burdens of the ministry will more quickly be spread and shared. This way the ministry capabilities of the church will be immeasurably broadened so that eventually more people, both of the problem and of the possibility varieties, can be touched. So splitting time between problem people and possibility people will not only lift the spirit, but lighten the load and thus preserve freshness for the far journey.

If your church grows as you hope it will, there will only be more and more "plates that need spinning." Yet, you are already facing more plates than one person can spin. It seems obvious then, that you cannot be the only minister in your church if it is to grow. And since it may not be feasible or possible at present to add a paid staff of "plate spinners," what are you going to do? If you are going to stay with your mission and stay fresh for the long haul something must give. So . . .

Delegate and Equip

Three, learn to spread the burdens of ministry by *delegating and equipping* possibility people. Delegating does not mean simply dumping jobs onto available bodies. Rather it means helping men and women discover and develop their own spiritual giftedness. It means you must delegate (1) meaningful tasks to others who have (2) spiritual gifts and passions suited to those tasks, then (3) equip them with skills to do those ministry tasks. Idle but gifted people ride the pews of nearly every congregation waiting for a challenge. But they will not be excited over busywork assignments, "so that they are involved." However they can become and remain excited about owning that part of the ministry dream which gives them opportunity to exercise their own unique giftedness.

The lives of most ministers could be enormously simplified by refining these two arts: delegating and equipping. As the members of a church feel a sense ownership of the church's mission and as they experience a sense of meaning and significance in their own efforts, a good deal of the "plate spinning" will be taken out of your hands. It will be spread around to others, who may indeed be far more suitably gifted than you are for many of the tasks you are now attempting.

Equipping and delegating, of course, are central to a minister's God-ordained job description. God gave some to be "evangelists, pastors, teachers," who are to "equip the saints for the work of the ministry," so that "the body of Christ might grow" (Eph. 4:11-13). When we work God's delegating and equipping agenda, we will not only take grinding burdens off our own backs but we will be working God's plan. In addition we will be laying the groundwork for an expanded and more effective churchwide ministry in the future.

Inventory Activities

Four, you might want to *inventory the activities expected* in your church. Most churches spin a number of old plates that don't really need spinning any more. With the passing of time, activities which may once have been very useful strategies may become only pointless but traditionally preserved events. As times change and your church develops a more specific focus to its purpose, these plates which no longer need spinning will become increasingly obvious. Gradually they can be gracefully retired, not just from your job description but from the congregational slate of "people eating" programs. Instead, let the church calendar be given to purposeful activities.

Planning

Five, *plan ahead*. An hour on Monday equals five on Friday. A week in January equals a month in July. While this principle applies to most aspects of our ministry, I am thinking specifically here of planning sermon series well ahead. This will not only de-escalate the stress and pressure of last minute sermon preparation, but significantly upgrade the quality of your preaching. But, how do we do this?

Earlier I said that I am partial to working my way through specific books of the Bible doing expository preaching. Here's my procedure in planning well ahead for *expository* series. However, I believe the same principles will apply to extended *topical* series as well.

(1) I begin focused and repeated reading of my intended book of the Bible, sometimes as much as a year in advance of a sermon series. Sometimes only a month or so.

(2) Early on, I block out the number of sermons required by a given book of the Bible, also fitting the available calendar time. Then I determine exactly what date each of these blocks of text will be preached. Here we underscore "blocks," to discourage the temptation to travel verse by verse. One series we did on the Gospel of John lasted nearly two years! Not only did we lose sight of John's point, but the church had long since grown weary. Besides, we probably read into John all sorts of things he never would have intended.

(3) Next, I create a separate file folder for each block of text. As my reading continues, I jot down insights on slips of paper and drop them in their appropriate files.

(4) As early as possible, I begin writing a "purpose statement" for each message and adding tentative titles as quickly as I can. This forces me to sharpen the focus of each message, although the focus may change several times before the actual day of preaching comes.

(5) During this extended preparation time, the book I am preaching feeds my own devotional life. This not only trims the bulk of my total

reading agenda, but helps focus my thought-power and passion. More importantly, I am forced to internalize this specific message in my own personal life, to attempt to live the sermons myself before I preach them to others.

(6) I glean from wider reading than "religious" material only. In fact, when the heart and mind become focused in a given series for several months, preparation of the series infuses my whole world of experience with a sense of intentionality. As insights and illustrations pop, I find myself saying, "All right! That fits in the message for, say, October the 10th." So I clip it or jot a note about it and drop it in the appropriate sermon file.

(7) Thus when the time arrives for actual outlining and crafting, I usually have far more than enough current and colorful material for every sermon.

Handmaidens of Joy

Of course, this process I have described presumes some specific habits as its handmaidens. These hearken back to the intentionality which is generated by a clear sense of purpose or mission. Some of the most obvious of these habits are as follows:

Read Widely

First, read widely from all kinds of writers, giving priority to literature of substance, both from the classic thinkers and the current minds. Also, read literature which helps you "understand the times," so that, like the men of Issachar, you will "know what Israel should do" (1 Chron. 12:32). Of course, wide reading takes time, which demands discipline. (Work and stress are two different things!) A lazy preacher will never be fresh. While some of his messages may be clever, even interesting, they will rarely be crisply on target, and they will lack that compelling ring of authenticity and urgency.

For me, discipline means rising early most mornings of my life, to cash in on those beautiful, high energy hours when the mind is fresh and creative, before feet walk, doors swing, and phones ring. This habit provides me five or six productive hours before noon. Of course, this also means I must be disciplined about the hour at which I go to bed. As Elton Trueblood says, "A lot of people ruin a good day the night before."[7]

Yes, I know my metabolism allows me to get by with less sleep than some. That is my rhythm. So don't attempt to imitate me or anyone else. You pick a time that fits you. But remember if you are to have ample reading time, you must attack the clock and calendar or they surely will attack you.

Listen Attentively

Second, listen attentively and systematically. Wherever I am, I want to be totally there. Someone has quipped, "You are nowhere unless you are where you are now!" Focus on now—the person in front of you now, the experience occurring now, the task confronted now.

To help you focus your attention and to preserve your gains for future usefulness, carry a notepad and jot things down. I have long since discovered one significant difference between those people who want to learn and grow and those who want merely to *appear* to be interested. People in the former category ask questions and seek sources and jot things down. The latter don't. When a person asks for my time, but never jots down book suggestions or key ideas, I feel frustrated. That person is quite often a "user" not a "grower." But systematic listening to every conversation, tape, trip, article, book, on ad infinitum, with attention focused and pad poised taps us into "Niagras of freshness."

Network Effectively

Third, use networking effectively. Students often ask me, "What is your most valuable ministry tool?" I reply, "It is not my experiences, my education, my library, my word processor, nor whatever God-given gifts I have received. No. It's my network." Across my thirty-five years of ministry my network of relationships with preachers, professors, professionals, businessmen, and other cutting-edge people has continually expanded. I genuinely value these relationships and I love and respect these people, doing my best to reciprocate resources.

Because of this treasured network of friendships, I am afforded near instant access to some of the best minds in our fellowship (and some outside) on a wide variety of subjects. Whenever a situation arises in which I don't know what to do (which is often), help is usually only a phone call or two away, because I know someone who knows what to do. And if I don't know who knows, I at least know "who knows who knows." These resource people are usually willing to share their expertise with me because we have cultivated mutual trust and affection, and because they also know that whatever resources I possess are always gladly theirs for the asking. So build relationships continually, nourish them lovingly and treat them with utmost respect. Your network will help keep you fresh and growing.

Play Regularly

Fourth, play regularly. Nothing re-creates like recreation, especially the kind that exercises the body. Not only does this give your mind a break, it also helps build a healthy body, which in turn provides more energy for the far journey. I run. The big payoff, however, is not physical, but emotional. I naturally seem to tend toward depression, which preys on weariness and stress. But with a good run, stress dissolves and my spirits soar. At many a low place, those alone miles running have meant my survival. They fed me freshness for the far journey.

Pray Fervently

Finally, pray fervently. The "steadfast love of the Lord," said Jeremiah, is "new every morning" (Lam. 3:23). One of the most beloved and eloquent preachers of our movement was T. B. Larimore of Alabama, who died in 1929. He was known for fresh and penetrating insight and for unparalleled flights of oratory. Once he was asked, "When do you think up those things?" and "How do you do it?"

Larimore is said to have replied, "Have you noticed those times when you see me sitting on the porch, looking out into the woods, and it would appear that I am doing nothing at all? Well, it is during those times that I think such thoughts and hear such words."

Larimore meant that those detached times were rich and fruitful seasons of reflection and prayer. During those interludes God released insight and creativity into him.

Open conversation with God with ample quiet reflection on His will and regular praise of His majesty is the surest and richest and most lasting "fountain of refreshment." Please don't let that last sentence slip by you as an expected platitude. I left it till the last of these suggestions, because good communication saves the punchline till last. Be careful: Because this can be said quickly and sounds familiar, do not let your heart miss the unlimited freshness found near the throne of God.

Endnotes for Section ❸

1. Quoted by Harry C. Howard, *Princes of the Christian Pulpit and Pastorate* (Nashville: Cokesbury Press, 1927), 250.

2. William Willimon, *Clergy and Laity Burnout* (Nashville: Abingdon Press, 1987), 25-26.

3. Viktor E. Frankl, *Man's Search for Meaning,* revised and updated, trans. Ilse Lasch (Boston: Washington Square Press, 1959), 12.

4. Stephen R. Covey, *The Seven Habits of Highly Effective People* (New York: Simon and Schuster, 1989), 65.

5. Covey, *Habits,* 95.

6. Eugene Peterson, *Working the Angles* (Grand Rapids: Eerdmans Publishing, 1987), 1-2.

SECTION
4

HOW CAN I GO
DEEP IN
SHALLOW TIMES?

For the time will come when men will not put up with sound doctrine. Instead, to suit their own desires, they will gather around them a great number of teachers to say what their itching ears want to hear. They will turn their ears away from the truth and turn aside to myths. But you, keep your head in all situations, endure hardship, do the work of an evangelist, discharge all the duties of your ministry.
2 Tim. 4:3-5

12

THE VANISHING ATTENTION SPAN

S ome time back I sat in a class as nationally-known radio preacher Charles Swindoll explained the nuts and bolts of his ministry. Someone asked, "Dr. Swindoll, why do we not see you on television?" Without hesitation Swindoll responded, "I am not sure the medium is compatible with the message." So we ask: Do the mass media superficialize the Gospel? Can a call to self-denial attract exhausted urbanites who turn to the tube for escape? Will a message dealing with life and death be taken seriously in an environment of sitcoms and overstated commercialism?

Behind those questions looms an even larger one: How can a comprehensive gospel, requiring time for deep reflection, be communicated in these hi-tech days of hurried people who are in love with the bottom line? We Americans sustain little interest in anything not obviously and directly connected with our felt needs. We like concrete better than abstract, and we would rather feel than think.

A Soft Market for Hard Truths

Yet (and here is the crunch), near the heart of the Christian faith lie some bedrock concepts which are not only quite abstract and cerebral but enormously demanding, as well.

In fact, some demands of the cross completely stand the culture on its head. Even in the most receptive and supportive church environments, some of this bedrock is not easily communicated. So, how can our preaching be both "big" and relevant at the same time? How do we get the abstract to the concrete? How indeed *do* we go deep in shallow times?

We preachers are feeling the pressure to "peddle our wares" quickly, before the audience's attention span runs out. After all, we know about "sound-bytes" and T.V. cameras changing angles every four seconds. So we abbreviate. And to "keep them coming back" we are tempted to lift from the Gospel only those most "marketable" features.

It is risky to tailor sermons to fit perceived human needs, without sound theological foundation. The preacher may make the folks in the pew feel good, but neglect the meat and potatoes of life, thus actually distorting the Gospel so that it is no longer really gospel. A market-driven, need-shaped gospel is not the everlasting Gospel of Christ. God is sovereign, thus His will is supreme. He is the center of all reality to whom all human life must relate and adjust or die. As Barth says, "We can come to God only through God Himself."[1]

Preaching That Connects

Yet, beware! For danger lurks at the other extreme. Fearing that relevant preaching will compromise their gospel, some preachers back out of touch with the times, into preaching which may be theologically sound, but does not connect with those who most need it. These preachers forget that theological themes are meant for real live people on specific streets.

A father was showing his young son the wonders of the city museum, when the lad spoke up rather loudly and said, "Dad, let's go someplace where the animals are real!"

They went to the zoo!

A museum is a great place to study the past, and there is nothing wrong with that; but most of us confess that the zoo is far more interesting.

Too often, we treat the Bible like a museum and do all of our preaching in the past tense. The sermon is a history lesson instead of an exciting encounter with the living God. We are museum guides, dusting off the artifacts and explaining the exhibits. While we are lecturing, our people are saying to themselves, "We wish we could go someplace where things are alive and real."

As Lischer put it, "Sermons are welded to interpersonal relationships."[2] Preaching must connect if it is to really be authentic preaching. Otherwise it is, at best, merely an exercise in irrelevance; at worst, an exercise in boredom.

So what indeed is a preacher to do? What will help us start preaching theological themes in the present tense, without losing eternity?

13

DANCING IN
MANY WORLDS

For years Carolyn and I have been trying to work out a fair division of responsibilities. I tell Carolyn, "I'll handle the big things, like whether Iraq should be allowed membership in the United Nations! You take care of the small stuff, like groceries, mortgage payments, and retirement." She seems to think I don't have a firm grasp on what "big" means. I guess "big" is in the eye of the beholder. When we attempt to preach deep things into shallow times, what is "big"? What theological themes should we classify as the "big" ones?

Profundity Can Be Simple

What's on your list? Predestination? Eschatology? Angelology? Premillennialism? Some of these will, of course, be difficult to connect with contemporary culture. Indeed, the sermon may be the wrong place to attempt such connection. Maybe the classroom or home Bible study setting would fit better. Preaching and teaching are not the same thing. But are topics like those listed above really the "big theological issues"? "Big" does not always mean complex or abstract.

The old story has it that after an erudite lecture by the legendary Karl Barth, a seminarian asked, "Doctor Barth, what is the most profound and lofty concept which your mind has ever brushed against?" Barth replied, "Jesus loves me this I know, for the Bible tells me so." The most simple is often the most significant.

In Scripture, a direct corollary runs between clarity and importance: The biggest theological concepts are pretty hard to miss! As was discussed in chapter six, Scripture clearly flags the "first importance" issues. The cross of Christ, of course, is the very central issue, followed by other big issues such as justice, mercy, trust, love, purity, servanthood, etc. However, these bedrock themes also present a tough communication challenge, not because they are complex to understand but because they are difficult to accept. They are not hard to see, just hard to swallow! So the trick in preaching these themes in our culture is not so much simplifying the complex or "concretizing" the abstract as it is slipping past the lines of defense into contemporary hearts and capturing the attention and penetrating the armor of the indifferent.

The Bible as Multi-Media

How does the Bible itself convey the "big" theological themes? Actually the lion's share of biblical communication is not linear sequential in nature, nor cerebral, nor informational. A lot of Scripture connects with human hearts at more affective and experiential levels than the intellectual alone. It connects from a variety of angles. Sometimes the Bible by-passes the brain and mainlines the message to the heart.

Aldous Huxley speaks of man as a "multiple amphibian." That is, we are constrained to make our way through many worlds at once (intellectual, emotional, aesthetic, sexual, psychological, social, cognitive, affective, etc.). But since the industrial revolution and with the more recent rise of the informational society, we have zeroed in on the linear sequential and production-oriented thought worlds. Thus, the "worlds" of information and production crowd out our "other worlds," (the more aesthetic and subjective human dimensions) which are atrophying. Consequently, Huxley believed, we are losing touch with what it means to be human.

Something similar could be said for faith which is grounded only in one kind of biblical world. When we attempt to analyze and explain God, Scripture becomes mere religious information and faith simply the progressive realization of moral or institutional goals. Could it be that we have so zeroed in on one dimension of revelation (the informational, propositional, didactic) and our "other worlds" have atrophied so that we are losing sight of much of what it means to believe?

Scripture Penetrates

God is too vast and mysterious for this purely cerebral use of Scripture. So are human beings. Scripture penetrates us on multiple levels with comprehensive and winsome force, reaching us at depths where propositional and informational truths don't go. This is precisely why Scripture contains so many literary genre and why preaching should, as well. The Bible speaks through drama, music, poetry, stories, paradox, and mystery, saying things that reach far beyond mere transmission of information.

Part of our communication problem solves itself when we preachers let each literary genre in Scripture speak for itself; that is, allow not only the content, but the style of the sermon to match the literary style of the text from which it is drawn. For example, something valuable is lost when we attempt a didactic sermon with rational, logical sequence from a section of poetry or story.

The full voice of our transcendent God dances through all of our worlds awakening them in ways too wonderful to explain and too sacred to be contrived. One of the joys of preaching which I most love is the awakening of the worlds! However, to preach large issues to the American culture leading into the twenty-first century in ways which waken all their worlds, demands not only creativity but serious, thoughtful preparation.

14

SETTING THE
CONCRETE

I n preparing a series on "big theological issues,"
first we will want to think theologically. This
does not mean thinking "fuzzily" nor abstractly.
But the more firmly and clearly we grasp the
"deep things of God" the easier it will be for us to
boil them down into popular language and connect them with felt needs. Thinking theologically
means reading Scripture in a fresh way. Learn to
look for the sweep of Scripture, rather than for
proof-texts from a constitution. Beware of raping
the text to force mere moralizing from it. Learn to
follow the story line of God's developing plot; to

feel the flow of God's mighty acts; and to trace repeated themes. Reading the Bible theologically means keeping an eye out for the things "of first importance."

A Strategy: Kingdom Theology for Consumers

While I have attempted for decades to preach theological themes so that the bread truck driver could connect with them, I had no clear rationale and strategy. But the doctor of ministry program forced an exercise upon me which turned out to be a God-send. I was assigned to preach a series on theological themes. But in preparation for that assignment, I had to write a major paper developing my rationale and strategy for the series.

"Exegeting" the Church

As the exercise unfolded, the Kingdom of God became the theological theme for my series. This theme came straight from the heart of our church. How? During the summer of 1989 we systematically "exegeted" the congregation. The elders and staff of the Highland church helped me catalogue the broad constituencies making up that large and pluralistic family. We then recruited representatives from these constituencies as "listeners" and trained them in a seminar to listen systematically through their social networks for felt needs. They were to catalogue what they heard and to suggest message themes in response.

Feedback came loud and clear: "Give us help in managing family stress: priorities, money, job, moral confusion, and change." In fact, one person phrased it, "How can I keep all the plates spinning? And if I can't, how do I decide which ones to drop?" (Does this question sound familiar?)

However, the "listeners" interpreted the felt needs which surfaced as merely symptoms pointing toward deeper problems of the heart; conditioned by a secular culture, many Christians at Highland, being saturated in a self-centered consumer culture, were actually (however unconsciously) wanting God for selfish purposes. The listeners perceived that a lot of our people seemed more interested in what they could get out of God (security, peace of mind, prosperity, self-actualization, etc.) than in what God wanted from them. Life was not lived to the glory of God, but God was being tapped for the glory of man.

The listeners convinced me that much of the family stress resulted from scrambled priorities; that our people didn't know how to prioritize things according to relative importance because they had no clear understanding of what was of utmost importance to them. Consequently, the listening groups and I (in a two-day reporting and planning retreat) determined to address the root of the problem, not merely the symptoms. In other words, the problem was actually "theological" rather than "situational." The listening group said, "Bottom line: Our people need to 'seek first the kingdom of God.'" (For them the "kingdom" of God is the "rule of God" in human hearts.)

Choosing the Text

Since we believed Kingdom Theology addressed the heart of the need, the Sermon on the Mount was chosen as the text because it capsules Kingdom Theology. The Sermon on the Mount refracts the "Kingdom light" from the whole Bible into the colors of practical, daily living.

Exegeting the Text

Once the theological theme and the text were chosen, the next step was careful exegesis of the text. Please note carefully: The text was chosen in the light of current congregational needs. So, in a sense, the exegesis of the congregation preceded the *choice* of texts. But we took great care to assure that felt needs did not *interpret* the text. We were determined not to shift our theological foundations. The Kingdom of God was to be the message preached! We knew we might be tempted to twist some facets of the Sermon on the Mount around to make them appear to be relevant. Thus we were adamant that exegesis of the text should stand above exegesis of the congregation, controlling the message, even though chronologically the congregation was "exegeted" prior to the exegesis of the text.

We acknowledged, of course, that "current situation" does inform understanding and application of the text. As Karl Barth would remind us, theology is always done in crisis. Theology which does not connect with real people is no theology. We also admitted that our human understanding of the text will always be somewhat distorted; colored by what we are experiencing when we open the Bible, no matter how honest our motives or how well we do our homework.

"Packaging"

Third, came the "packaging" of the "big" issues. (This may be the toughest part of preaching that goes deep in shallow times.) Our aim was to project Kingdom theology from the Sermon on the Mount into the lives of the people at Highland, in their heart-language. Our means: to package Kingdom theology in attractive units that connect with their issues and experiences.

Packaging begins with titles. Good titling helps three ways: It helps the preacher target his message with precision. Titles help communicate the message, and creative titles can actually help attract listeners. So, our titles attempted to stretch from life-setting to text.

Since the media has conditioned the people on our pews to communication by imaging, rather than through laborious thoughtfulness, we avoided titles which sounded text-centered. For example, a title like, "What does the Bible say about the Kingdom of God? Studies from Matthew 5:1—7:29," may be technically accurate. But it sounds boring. It makes no connection with the felt needs of the audience. So, we called the series, "Wings for Weary Families." This title begins not with the text, but with the felt needs of the church. "Wings" was our metaphor for Kingdom perspective on life, and "weary families" picked up on the felt need.

Meeting Them Where They Are

We assumed too that a lot of our folks would find difficulty making connection between abstract, theological truths and concrete, personal daily living. But we also knew there can be no

"Wings for the Weary" unless they tap into Kingdom truth. Yet Kingdom truth cannot be understood without some serious reflection and rigorous thought.

To further complicate matters, when Kingdom truth does get through, it is threatening. A call to yield up self-interest and be "poor in spirit," meek, hungry, to mourn, to suffer, to give, and to turn the other cheek in self-denial does not sound very attractive to the consumer mentality of our times. Thus we did not expect straightforward deductive lectures on abstract Kingdom principles to connect with our people. Instead we chose an indirect or deductive strategy, which Craddock would call "overhearing the Gospel." So our approach, while expository in content, was to be *inductive* in style. That is, we wanted to begin each sermon with the specific felt needs and common experiences and bridge back to Kingdom theology which applies to those needs and experiences. To lead our church toward theological "depths," we began in felt need "shallows." We believed that if we started at the other end of the bridge, the theological end, we would at best lose our listeners' attention and at worst drive them away.

But, beware of a market-driven message. Again, I emphasize that this approach must not allow theology to be shaped by human need. Rather, this strategy understands that the significance of Kingdom theology will more likely get through to people who see a real connection between "Kingdom" and the stuff they face when they walk out of the church building. Of course, some industrial strength theological concepts cannot be expounded through overhearing and induction, but will require a didactic form of

communication. Preaching may not be the best forum for this kind of material, however. As mentioned earlier, didactic material may be better
suited to the classroom than to the pulpit. Yet, an
inductive approach in the pulpit can prepare the
church for *deductive* teaching in the classroom.

Kingdom Living

During my assigned series, the messages
aimed to remind the "weary" that "blessings" are
available only through Kingdom Living which in
turn is for the poor in spirit. But while we hooked
the church through their felt need for relief from
the bewildering and fatiguing pressures of money,
family, job, friends, success, community, church,
etc., each sermon ultimately insisted that personal relief is not the Christian objective. Kingdom is! Personal relief and blessing are merely
by-products of "seeking, knocking, and asking" for
the rule of God through Jesus.

On a practical level, each sermon assumed
that most stress results from over-scheduling due
to scrambled priorities. However, when the kingdom is first, the relative importance of other issues becomes clear. Thus, "Kingdom wings" help
"weary families" to arrange their priorities less
stressfully.

Using the first sermon in the series on "Wings
for Weary Families," let me illustrate the principles I have stated so far in this section. The title
of that sermon is "Who Is Driving Your Bus?" The
gist of this first sermon was as follows:[3]

Family life is often wearying. But some
family stress may be self-inflicted because too

much emphasis is placed upon family as the focal point of life and spiritual well-being.

If we start the train before we get our people on board, we can hardly expect them to travel with us toward our destination. To bring our people along with us to the theological theme of "Kingdom," we attempted to get them on board by beginning with their feelings and experiences. I have no statistical proof, but I believe that at least 50% of the expository sermons preached in America last Sunday started with, "Now, if you have your Bibles, please turn to . . . ." The other 50% began with, "Now, you'll remember that last week we discussed . . . ."

So, in this sermon, rather than beginning with something like, "Open your Bibles" or "The Sermon on the Mount has good things to say to you who are under stress and don't know where to turn," the sermon began with an attention riveting felt need story, as follows:

A San Antonio attorney made headlines recently. Everything in this man's life was full of promise. He led a new and already flourishing practice. He had just begun a new marriage with a bright, beautiful, adoring wife. They had recently moved into a new house and had driven home a new car a few days earlier. But on Friday, this young lawyer headed home from the office, rolled into the driveway, walked inside the house, crawled into a sleeping bag, and shot himself to death. He left a note for his bride, "It isn't that I don't love you, I just feel so tired."

The sermon went on,

All of us sometimes feel nearly this weary, especially those responsible for the care of a family. But, could it be that we sometimes make a bigger deal out of family living than what God intended?

The message then shifted to an apocryphal letter written from some parents to their friends describing a family tragedy, a son gone wrong:

> We don't understand it. He is a bright student and a fine athlete. He has risen fast in the military and was looking forward to law school. His future is unlimited, some even talk of high office one day. But recently he joined some eastern religious sect and turned his back on his past life, even his family, it seems. He has no time for us because he spends it all with his "religious brothers and sisters." His whole ambition seems now, to serve them and his cause. He has even broken off with his fiance, who was devastated (so are we) and says he plans never to marry. Our whole family is heartsick, and we don't know what to do.

> Question: Who was this? The Moonies? Hari-Krishna? The Boston Church? Actually, it could have been many a young first century Christian: John Mark or Apollos—or the apostle Paul.

The sermon then noted that

> family is a hot topic these days, but more questions need to be asked about it. The "dangerous" biblical texts raise some frightening issues which are often overlooked at family enrichment seminars. In fact, some of Jesus' comments seem almost antithetical to family life!

At this point I read, without comment, some of the strong statements from Jesus like, "A man's enemies will be the members of his own household" (Matt. 10:36), "Anyone who loves his father or mother more than me is not worthy of me"

(Matt. 10:37), and "They will be divided, father against son and son against father" (Luke 12:53), etc.

After reviewing the radical demands of Jesus, which seem on the surface to militate against family life (Luke 9:59-62; 12:50-53; 14:26), we observed that, while not all believers are required to leave their families, all *are* called to put the kingdom first.

Kingdom Priority

Along with the central text from Matthew 6:33, the vignette from Mark 3:31-35 was then explored:

> Jesus' distraught family stood outside the house, calling to Him, thinking that His rejection of them was because He was "out of His mind." They wanted to "get the family back together." Jesus insisted, however, that His real family was the circle of followers in the house, who were held together, not so much by the bonds of blood kinship, but by a common higher priority, the transcendent commitment of Kingdom. For Jesus, nuclear family was important, but not ultimate.

The application section of this sermon suggested:

> Without Kingdom priority, when a family focuses upon its own preservation and fulfillment, the resulting expectations are too much for the family to bear. The family was not meant to receive life's total focus, nor to be assigned life's highest value. Family cannot provide ultimate security or complete happiness and fulfillment. The family will not last forever. Thus the family does not call for our

highest ultimate loyalties. Rather, "Seek first the Kingdom."

Kingdom Resources

However, we then moved our listeners to more positive family implications of Kingdom living:

> When the rule of Christ becomes the focus which transcends family, then family life becomes less demanding, possessive, jealous, and protective. In seeking the Kingdom, "all these things are added." Only in the Kingdom are adequate resources available for fulfilling family living. Only Kingdom loyalty uprights our priorities to ease unnecessary stress. Only Kingdom power provides the strength to bear the unavoidable stresses. Only when "the love of God is poured into our hearts" can real love reign in our families.

Local Illustrations

This particular sermon's application was then illustrated from our local setting. The Highland church supports Brian and Becky Gibbs in Brazil. Brian is the son of one of our elders, J.B. Gibbs. So we asked,

> What if J. B. and Winnie Gibbs had said, "We can't bear for Brian and Becky to live in Rio. Our family solidarity is too important"?

Also, our own son Christopher and his friend Jeff Salmon had just spent three months doing relief work in Haiti, the poorest country in the western hemisphere. So I said,

> Yes, we parents would have enjoyed having Jeff and Chris safe at home this summer. But it means a lot more that they were in Haiti— not nearly so safe, but much more "splendid."

Yes, it would mean a lot to me and Carolyn (and all of us parents) if our kids lived in Abilene, and we could see them any time we want. But what means much more is that they are serving people and honoring God where they are—*that* will live on.

Kingdom Unity

Toward the conclusion of the sermon we pointed out that,

> In the end, Kingdom priorities bring families great enrichment and harmony after all, by uniting family members in a common higher cause, with more substantial love, in a lasting framework—the Church, which is extended family. Thus family enrichment is a *by-product* of Kingdom living, not the *central life objective*. As short time stewards of marriage, family, and children, we will not be measured by how stress-free family life is, but by whether we are God's instruments to prepare family members toward "the purpose for which they came into the world." Here is the most important family question: "Is family lived out to Kingdom glory and usefulness?" Not, "Is my life stress-free with Sunday dinners together?" The world will little note nor long remember whether my family enjoyed family life, but it will be impacted eternally if my children live lovingly, courageously, and unselfishly."

As the rest of the series progressed, each sermon carried a hint of hope ahead and some possible next steps, while avoiding pat answers. The bridge from life to text moved lesson upon lesson to apply an expansive view of Kingdom in practical ways to daily life on the streets of

Abilene.[4] Repeat: Thinking theologically definitely does not mean irrelevant thinking.

When the assigned series was completed, the congregation evaluated it in the light of previous series. In every category, this Kingdom series rated higher than most previous series. A clear rationale and strategy for preaching theological themes helped this preacher go "deep in shallow times."

Prepare Expositionally

As I asserted earlier, I am partial to expository preaching. Yes, the *target* of good preaching may rise out of the current needs of the congregation, but in the long haul, the *purpose* must arise out of the Word of God (which, incidentally, is always current). I want my sermons to be expository, at least in *source*, if not in *genre*.

No, expository preaching does not necessarily mean the sequential study of some large section of Scripture. Rather the term "expository" simply refers to sermons sourced in the text. Whenever the text is fairly exegeted (even a fragment of it) and projected into the current life situation, expository preaching is taking place.

Topical preaching, on the other hand, is selecting a topic, then developing that topic with several texts, while allowing the topic to shape the message. Of course, "topical" preaching is a valid preaching genre, provided the texts which develop the topic are used fairly.

However, as explained in chapter six, I definitely prefer extended series of sermons from a big chunk of text. This gives the text more opportunity to shape the message. Also, I believe longer preparation and reflection do a better job of bridging the message of the text to the lives of the people.

A procedure for expository preparation was outlined in chapter eleven. We merely summarize it here:

One, begin reading and re-reading the book months ahead of time, gradually dividing it into natural "blocks" of material.

Two, look for the point of the book and then determine how each block of text contributes toward it.

Three, project the point of each block into current settings.

Four, as soon as possible, prepare a folder for each block. Then in a sentence or two, write the thrust for the sermon and give each sermon block a tentative title. Such sentences and titles will force your sermons to get specific and intentional early on. As the months of reading continue, accruing insights can be jotted down and dropped into the appropriate folders. This, along with illustrations and insights from all other sources, will bring you to the day of actual outlining with far more than enough fresh and targeted material.

Five, try to let the text itself shape both the *content* of the message, and as far as possible, the *structure* of the sermon. Through this process you will be well on your way to "intentionality," the next important factor in preaching theological themes to contemporary audiences.

Prepare Intentionally

Be sure to prepare intentionally; that is, give the sermon a clear objective. The preacher must preach because he has "something to say," never simply because he is "expected to say something."

When the actual day to craft the sermon arrives, I ask myself:

- Is this message in here just because I wanted to cover this interesting passage?
- Is it just to fill a thirty-minute time slot?
- To hold the crowd?
- To hold my job?
- To say the truth?
- Or does it have some clear and significant strategic purpose: to connect the "big theological issue" of this block of Scripture with specific spiritual needs in this local church at this point in time?

So That . . .

"Big" issues are never to be addressed for the purpose of information alone. They are to be preached "so that!"

- So that people might see God. To adore Him, fear Him, and have their hearts broken over the things that break His heart.
- Or *so that* they might serve Him and glorify Him.

- Or *so that* people will see Jesus; *so that* they will be changed into his likeness.

- Or *so that* the Great Physician can heal their brokenness, or give strength in trial or comfort in suffering.

The sermon must always be preached *so that* men and women can see how the "big theological issues" are connected to life at its daily experiential level.

Plan of Action

However, while good preaching is intentional, its intent is not to "do a number" on people. Sermons must not be preached merely to raise money, raise attendance, whip out indifference, control morality, or manipulate performance. Paul soundly renounced such "shameful" use of the pulpit, calling it "deception" and "distort[ion of] the word of God" (2 Cor. 4:2). But, at the same time, a sermon on "big issues" connects best when it calls for a specific plan of action. For example, the sermons on "Wings for Weary Families" called for a specific, concrete shift in priorities, parenting styles, and budget line items, etc.

Intentionality also means that when a preacher calls for a definite plan of action, he should have machinery in place for clear steps toward this action. Otherwise frustration will result, and eventually calls to action will be ignored not because people do not want to respond, but because they do not know "how" to take "what" specific first steps.

For example: For years I preached on substance abuse in our church, challenging people to "deal with their alcohol and drug problems." However, I was never specific about the action, because we had no machinery in place to assist them. So even people who were convicted by those messages did little to act on them. But now, thanks to the ministry of Bill Nash and others, the Highland church offers a variety of biblically based twelve-step groups which have aided many in recovery from addictions and compulsions. Now, I can preach at that church with much clearer intentionality. I can encourage substance abusers to join a group. I can tell them who, where, when, and how. Part of your "sermon preparation" may need to be the designing of means to implement your sermon. Then the preaching can "go deep in shallow times."

When we *think theologically, prepare expositionally*, and *preach with intentionality*, having a clear objective in mind and machinery in place for the first practical steps, "big theological themes" will more readily connect with people conditioned by "consumerism" and selfishness.

15

BREAKING THE SILENCE

Finally comes the moment of truth: delivering the sermon. Most of the preacher's work is best done in silence. The best listening requires silence. Study is silent. Prayer is often in silence. Reflection is in silence. But, as the preacher approaches the pulpit to break the silence, he wonders: Will my words be any improvement over the silence?

How do we deliver the message? How do we dare speak the massive truths out loud?

Speak From Experience

First, it helps to speak from experience! If I have experienced direct personal confrontation with the issue of the hour my words will more likely bear the ring of truth. As Moses E. Lard said, back in 1849,

> Think, my dear young preaching brother, think of your subject; think of it till your head aches and your heart is clear; think till you cannot make a blunder; think till every point is transparent, luminous; think till the mind bounds over it, and plays about with the ease of a gamboling fawn.[5]

For years I have been painfully aware that if I have not internalized the message, if I have not lived this truth before I speak it, at best I will only be giving a lecture. At worst, I will further contribute to the crisis of trust.

But if I have felt my story connect with the big point of His story, and if my story overlaps the stories of the people who hear me, my message can bridge theology to life experience in an authentic way; my message will connect! My words will be an improvement over the silence.

Involve the Church

Second, involve the church. Difficult "meat and potatoes" material will be digested more easily if everyone "chews" on the stuff, if the whole church is involved in the communication process. At Highland we often designed "whole church" series. One example would be a series we did on Nehemiah entitled "The Wall: Building Belonging Among the People of God." We did not rely on the preaching alone to carry the freight. Rather, we loaded the cargo on a number of wagons. For starters, besides the sermons, we also drew the classes into the process.

On Wednesday nights, John Willis, one of the elders, equipped the Sunday adult teachers with heavy backup material to guide the classes which met after the morning worship. The sermons initiated a link from theology to life. But the classes were designed to discuss and internalize the practical implications introduced by the sermons.

Children's classes participated in drama and music which drew from the Nehemiah story suitable applications for each age level. The children also built a "Nehemiah's Wall" across the front of the auditorium. Each child created a block with the child's name on it to symbolize his or her place among the people of God. And then on Sunday morning, the children publicly placed the block in the wall. God taught these children valuable lessons as they reenacted building Nehemiah's wall.

Individual families also became involved in the communication process. Each family was supplied reading guides and discussion questions, encouraging home devotionals from Nehemiah to parallel the preaching.

In addition, Sunday worship experiences were carefully planned around the "big" Nehemiah themes being addressed from the pulpit. Occasional special pageantry in the auditorium highlighted themes in festive style, stirring enthusiasm in the church. Musically gifted members of our church wrote special songs which were either sung to the congregation or learned by the congregation. Short, well-done dramatic skits aided at certain points, not only supplying another medium of communication, but involving more persons and gifts in the total communication environment.

Also, we handed out sermon notes to everyone at the beginning of each service. These helped listeners track with me as I slogged through the heavy places. The notes also listed related passages for further exploration, and fill-in-the-blanks sections involved the congregation physically, helping to stretch their attention spans.

Transcendence

Third, speak with transcendence. Warren Weirsbe tells a story about a preacher who was delayed in getting to a meeting. Seeing this, Satan got there first and told the people he was the substitute. He opened the pulpit Bible and proceeded to preach. The preacher finally arrived, recognized Satan in the pulpit, and was amazed to hear him declaring biblical truth.

After the meeting, the preacher said to the Devil, "Weren't you afraid to preach the truth of God's word, lest it weaken your own kingdom?"

Satan smiled and replied, "My preaching won't change anybody's life. You see, I can speak the right words, but I don't have any unction!"

But you ask, "Lynn, what did he mean by unction?" Well, I agree with the legendary country preacher who said, "I can't tell you *when* unction is, but I can sure tell you *when* it ain't!"[5]

And, preacher, this "unction" begins in your own hours alone in *private* worship! If we do not bring the overflow of personal worship into the corporate gathering, our public attempts at worship may only result in what Paul Faulkner calls "the dry heaves" as we try to bring up from within us something that isn't there. People can sense whether the preacher before them is a private worshipper, not by subtle boasting, or word-dropping about journaling, etc., but by his very bearing.

When this "unction" rests on the preacher, its presence is unmistakable, like it was one evening when Landon Saunders, nationally-known radio voice, rose to speak at a highly charged key conference. Something beyond description marked his whole being. Audience buzz automatically quieted, and every eye seemed riveted on Landon. Glen Owen, an elder sitting next to me, leaned over and whispered in my ear, "He glows as if he had just stepped from the throne room." Landon's private worship was spilling over into our public gathering. Was that "unction"?

Thus, we bring our *private* worship to our preaching in the context of *corporate* worship. And preaching is itself an act of worship! Sermons are preached to people, yes. But each sermon is also offered as a sacrificial lamb to God. At every stage of the preparation and of the delivery—even the afterglow (or aftermath, as the case may be)— preaching is richest when it is regarded by both preacher and congregation as an act of adoration and worship to God. Yet preaching is only one factor in the whole equation of corporate worship.

Adoration

Rich corporate worship begins with *adoration*. I worship and preach much better when the worship period begins with enthusiastic praise addressed directly to God. Scripture says that

God inhabits the praise of His people, so we must draw near to God and exalt His name. Such a season of moving prayer and praise in rich worship also elevates a congregation to a heightened sense of readiness for the preaching of the Word. In worship, God comes to us and speaks to us, not just we to Him.

Intentional

Also, the best of corporate worship is *intentional.* Songs should not be sung merely as "filler" or to "quiet the audience." This not only distracts from worship, but it actually trains the congregation to sing hymns without contemplating their meaning. Hymns, readings, prayers, sermon, and all other worship ingredients should gather around a central and specific theme, not just God in general. For example, each individual Sunday hour of worship could zero in on a facet of God, such as: Holiness, Majesty, Creator, Judge, Steadfast Love, Healer, Provider, etc.

All elements of worship aid each other if their themes are interwoven. So preaching is greatly enhanced by clear coherence among all the elements of a worship assembly. It keeps the congregation focused, rather than leading them on emotional or intellectual rabbit chases. As we preach the deep themes in our shallow times, we help internalize the message by approaching each theme through several worship media.

Sense of Flow

Worship is also enriched by a *sense of flow.* That is, ingredients of worship are most meaningful if they lead smoothly from one to the next. Our people often come in to worship still tense and distracted from scurrying around their dressing rooms or hurrying through the streets to their pews. They need time and an intentional process to help lead them first to calmness and then to the throne of God. Just as theaters have lobbies and church buildings have foyers to transition people from one mode to another, even so worship periods need prelude, intentionality, and flow.

One of the most common atrocities perpetrated against worship in our traditional assemblies is that we keep interrupting ourselves. Rather than having a season of praise, where one hymn or song leads intentionally to the next, coherently carrying the worshipper in a specific direction, we tend to be disjointed. Sing. Stop. Announce a song. Sing. Stop. Read. Stop. Announcements. Humor. Pray. Stop. Sing. We thus inhibit the flow. When worship has a sense of flow, the preaching will be empowered by the rest of the worship and will itself be a more authentic act of worship.

Heart Language

Not just the preaching, but the entire worship experience is strongest when it *connects with the heart language* of as many congregational constituencies as possible. A patchwork of differing kinds of people walk into most of our assemblies each Sunday. In the light of this, the worship planning group in our church systematically draws a grid of age levels and cultural backgrounds. Each week we ask ourselves, what ingredient of this plan will connect with singles, or blue-collar, or white-collar, or youth, or academics, or business people, etc.? Each of these subgroups will "speak" its own unique "heart language." Some are right-brained; some, left-brained; some like contemporary music, some classical. Some like stories, some are linear thinkers. Some like quietness, others thrive on raucous involvement. This illustration will appeal to one group, that one to another.

Of course, in a heterogeneous church we cannot expect to connect with every group every Sunday. But we study our grid and ask ourselves as we plan each week: Whose comfort zones have we violated too many times in a row? What constituencies were left out of the heart language last week? What do they need this week to feel emotional ownership of the worship experience?

The sermon must pass through this "grid" as well. An issue of importance to one segment of the congregation may be irrelevant or "old hat" to another. Even the style of communication and the type of illustrations used should alternate among the "heart languages" of the various constituencies within the congregation.

Yet, at least some sermons should stretch people! Yes, it is treacherously easy to preach over people's heads, but I am convinced that I must not be afraid to challenge people. I do not mean "make a concept as difficult to follow as possible," but good preaching gradually expands the capacity of a church and elevates its levels of interest. "Stretching concepts" can be skillfully woven into most sermons in ways that stimulate the advanced thinker to go further, yet without losing the attention of the less advanced thinker. So, in each sermon, I try to include some feature for each of as many constituencies in the congregation as possible.

Among the People

When we rise to preach, we stand with the sinners as one of them, not apart from them or above them. I personally find myself in an ongoing struggle to consciously and consistently remind myself to preach from this posture. This means many things. For example, "we" vocabulary might replace "I" words, wherever possible.

Vulnerability

Also, vulnerability, which describes spiritual struggles in current terms, places us in more authentic relationship with our people. Carefully chosen stories which appropriately reveal our own personal foibles might be used as illustrations, at least as frequently as our personal victory stories.

This must be carefully thought through, however, as Henri Nouwen warns,

> On the one hand, no minister can keep his own experience of life hidden from those he wants to help. Nor should he want to keep it hidden. While a doctor can still be a good doctor even when his private life is severely disrupted, no minister can offer service without a constant and vital acknowledgment of his own experiences. On the other hand, it would be very easy to misuse the concept of the wounded healer by defending a form of spiritual exhibitionism. A minister who talks in the pulpit about his own personal problems is of no help to his congregation, for no suffering human being is helped by someone who tells him that he has the same problems. Remarks such as, "Don't worry because I suffer from the same depression, confusion, and anxiety as you do," help no one. This spiritual exhibitionism adds little faith to little faith and

creates narrow-mindedness instead of new perspectives. Open wounds stink and do not heal.[6]

Making one's own wounds a source of healing, therefore, does not call for a sharing of superficial personal pains but for a constant willingness to see one's own pain and suffering as rising from the depth of the human condition which all men share.

Compassionate Illustrations

Our illustrations connect best when they rise out of our local community of faith and reveal the preacher's understanding of and compassion for personal current realities, and it really helps when our homegrown illustrations affirm our people.

Even as I am preparing a sermon, it helps me to picture real people, imagining exactly where they are and what they are doing, thinking, feeling at the moment I am preparing the lesson. I envision what their facial expression or body language might say when I hit this or that point in the sermon. I ask myself questions like:

- Will the tone of these comments on the consequences of divorce crush and pigeonhole divorced people and their children, or will these comments heal and help?

- Will that family who lost a son hear my comments on causes of suicide as compassionate empathy with struggling parents, or might my words crush them? Will I risk being heard as accuser or judge?

• Will my manner of addressing
  abortion devastate the college girl
  who has just gone through one?

And so on.

Of course, a preacher's tone of voice betrays
his heart. I constantly knock on the Father's door
in prayer, begging Him for a heart of genuine compassion that will come through in the tenderness
of my words and voice.

Passionate Preaching

When abstracts hit the concrete, when theology touches people we love and in whom we have
investment, passion rises. This is the point at
which we recall looks in eyes, body language,
words in the hall, faces at the rim of the conversation, tears falling on the carpet of our study floor,
laughter over a shared burst of insight, even
angry exchanges—and passion wells up within us.
Interestingly, I rarely find myself feeling such
passion as a guest speaker addressing strangers.
These are family passions, the passions of lovers.
And the deeper the relationship runs with the
people, the more passionate the delivery becomes.
But, authentic passion flows out of generous
amounts of time, often painfully invested in the
lives of the people who sit before our pulpits.

In its purest form, however, passion flows
from the glory of the cross. The preacher who
glories in the cross will passionately desire to lead
his church to the cross with him. "Get them in
sight of Calvary," said A. J. Gossip in his lectures
on preaching. "Pause there . . . hushed and
reverent; enable them to look, to see it, make
it real to them, not just an old tale that has

lost its wonder and its stab, but a tremendous awful fact."[7]

When the Holy Spirit inhabits targeted prayer and praise in the preparation and delivery of a sermon, He brings passion. Scripture promises that He has "poured out his love into our hearts" (Rom. 5:5). Frequently, just before stepping to the pulpit, I find myself praying, "Lord, pour Your love into my heart. Help me to genuinely love the people sitting here today, not just to love with my will but with my emotions." And God is faithful. He brings "tenderness and compassion" (Phil. 2:1).

Sunday has come. The lights in the sanctuary are up. The people of God are gathering. Relationships run deep between preacher and church. The preparation has been thorough. The preacher knows the searing current of the hot wire of God's word. He stands in the shadow of the cross. He also knows the life-sapping drain of the ground-wire of human need. He passionately and tenderly loves his people. And so he stands amidst the profoundly rich atmosphere of thoughtful, joyful worship. The *deep* things of God are about to connect with God-hungry pilgrims traveling through *shallow* times.

As he opens his mouth to speak, the preacher closes the circuit. He is now *on* the cross. For God's sake. What agony. What glory. What mystery. What freshness! For God's sake.

Endnotes for Section ❹

1. Karl Barth, as quoted by Robert W. Duke, *The Sermon as God's Word: Theologies for Preaching* (Nashville: Abingdon, 1980), 15.

2. Richard Lischer, *A Theology of Preaching: The Dynamics of the Gospel* (Nashville: Abingdon, 1981), 29.

3. Sermon series preached at Highland Church of Christ, Abilene, Texas, Fall 1989.

4. Robert Lynn Anderson, *Congregational Participation in the Preparation, Delivery, and Evaluation of a Sermon Series: An Abstract of a Project Thesis Presented to the Graduate School,* Abilene Christian University, Doctor of Ministry, February 1990.

5. Warren Weirsbe, "Unction," Prokop'e Newsletter, VI, 2 (March-April 1989).

6. Henri J. Nouwen, *The Wounded Healer,* as quoted in *A Guide to Prayer for Ministers and Other Servants* (Nashville: The Upper Room, 1983).

7. A. J. Gossip, "The Preaching of the Cross."

SECTION

5

HOW DO I KNOW WHEN IT'S TIME TO GO?

Section 5 is an edited version of my article "Why I've Stayed," Leadership 7 (Summer 1986):76-82. Used by permission.

16

LONG-PLAYING RECORD

Randy, a fellow minister and friend, caught my eye and motioned toward a private corner. I could see a heavy question coming. "How do you know when it is time to move?" he almost begged.

His searching eyes suggested the question was more painfully complex than its simple phrasing. Randy is not alone. Most ministers find themselves in his quandary periodically, if not persistently.

For nearly twenty years I served one church, but I frequently faced the question of moving. I am not suggesting ministers should never move. A move is sometimes imperative. And, indeed, I finally moved last year. Over those two decades, however, I chose to stay because of some guidelines hammered out along the way. These principles at least brush against the question Randy and you and I often ask: Is it time to move?

No doubt you sense my bias. I am unabashedly in favor of long tenures in ministry. Ministry, like marriage, finds its fulfillment in faithfulness. Marriage vows are intended to last until death brings separation. Of course, a ministerial covenant does not imply such sacred permanence; nevertheless, when a "shepherd" is called to a covenant with a "flock," that union is not to be terminated lightly.

The Long-Playing Record

Longevity in ministry is an enormous plus. After nearly twenty years with the same church, I have observed:

- The first two years you can do nothing wrong.

- The second two years you can do nothing right.

- The fifth and sixth years of a ministry, either you leave, or the people who think you can do nothing right leave. Or you change, or they change, or you both change.

- Productive ministry emerges somewhere in the seventh year or beyond.

Rapport

Why does increasing tenure generally enrich
the quality of ministry? For one thing, time gives
the sensitive minister intimate rapport with the
community. He sees its needs more clearly. The
minister also becomes more familiar with the
local communication networks. Thus, in most
cases, time helps a minister connect more precisely with the needs of the people.

Effective ministry often demands that a
church make costly and radical shifts. Even the
most loyal Christians will not willingly retool
major patterns of living in response to temporary
pulpit leadership. But when godly people gain
confidence in the permanence of a leader and
accept the direction he is going, they will more
readily make the significant changes necessary.

Example: Some years back at Highland we
were facing the possibility of a major building project. Even before the findings were complete, the
elders wanted to know if they could reasonably expect me to be in the Highland pulpit for at least
the next five years. Was I indispensable to the
growth of that church? Definitely not! Today, under Mike Cope's gifted preaching, Highland is en-
joying her best days yet. But back then, the
people were being asked to pay the high price of
expansion in dollars, work, and inconvenience. Before they could be expected to make such commit-
ments, they deserved some assurance that there
would be no switch of signals from the pulpit.

Credibility

Long tenure in ministry also enhances credibility. People respect and trust a person who loves

them. Only over time can love be authenticated.
I've believed this a long time, but I believe it even
more since M. J.'s wedding.

M. J. grew up in our congregation. She
started first grade the year I arrived. She was
part of our youth ministry, mission trips, and singing groups. M. J.'s parents are divorced. I often
listened and prayed as she processed the pain of
family problems. Once M. J. went as our "daugh-
ter" on a churchwide family canoe trip down the
Guadalupe River.

During the hours of premarital counseling
with M. J. and Mark, they penetrated my heart
even deeper. Then came the wedding, a garden af-
fair under the oaks and amid the flowers. While
the wedding was informal, it had a touch of ele-
gance. The bridal attendants were Libby, Carra,
Marla, and Holly—friends M. J. had grown up
with. As little girls they had skipped into Sunday
School together with their bashful gap-toothed
grins and white stockings that sometimes bagged
at the knees.

At one point during the ceremony, all the girls
sang the words from Jeremiah 31:12-13:

> They will come and shout for joy on the
> heights of Zion;
> they will rejoice in the bounty of the Lord. . . .
> Then maidens will dance and be glad, young
> men and old as well.
> I will turn their mourning into gladness;
> I will give them comfort and joy instead of
> sorrow.

For a few seconds, I heard the voices of little
girls singing, and the rush of emotion was nearly
frightening. I was scarcely able to gather my

scattered wits to continue the ceremony. Oh, yes! Powerful feelings flow between church and minister that only time can generate.

A healthy family in the "parsonage" also enhances the minister's credibility. As a minister's family moves successfully through several developmental stages before the watching eyes of the community, the leaders of that family gather respect as parents who manage relationships well and whose faith is authentic enough to be contagious.

Awesome Access

The access to people's lives during a long tenure of ministry is awesome. A teacher sees a child in a handful of classes at best. A coach will relate to athletes for one or two seasons. A counselor or social worker or policeman will see a few people, and then only when they are in trouble. But God's minister enjoys interaction with staggering numbers of people of all ages and through a collage of experiences and changes. Life-changing impact continues as long as both preacher and people remain in the same congregation, and even beyond.

The Sunday morning prior to high school graduation is traditionally a roller coaster of emotions at our church. The seniors sit in a special section. I usually step over to where they're seated and reminisce a bit with each one, then give some personal words of blessing and farewell. The elders present each senior with a signed New Testament and give each student a warm, often tearful hug and a heartfelt prayer.

In my twelfth year at Highland, Senior Sunday hit me with hurricane strength. As I looked into the faces of more than thirty young men and women, I was suddenly overwhelmed by the realization that their lives and mine had been entwined since they were in first grade.

I had screamed at their ball games, grieved with some through death or divorce in their families, talked one or two down from drug and alcohol binges, and heard whispered confessions of fear of pregnancy. We had been canoeing, backpacking, and swimming together. I had spoken at school events, even hugged track stars and homecoming queens and their friends. I had heard most of them confess Jesus as Lord and had baptized a number of them. And now they were leaving! What those kids and I were feeling—what the whole church was feeling—is just a small slice of the ministry possible only through long tenure.

Many factors enter the minister-church relationship as time passes. I can enumerate only a few here. But one thing is sure: eventually, these elements combine in a powerful synergism not attainable in a few years. The ministry with the most impact is usually the one that has survived the longest. All too often, hasty moves cut short what could have been an increasingly rewarding ministry.

17

A TIME TO STAY

Before we discuss specific reasons to go or to
stay, we need to lay a foundation. My assumptions about minister-church relationships distill
into three words: calling, shepherd, and covenant.

Calling

First, what is a calling? Do you not yearn for a
task of God's choosing rather than your own,
something bearing a divine aura? I know I do. But
a sense of calling, while indispensable, is also vulnerable to self-deception. Calling is claimed
through a wide variety of experiences—from the
traditional to the bizarre.

The story is told that deep in the jungle, at a fork in the road, sat a witch doctor, his weathered face locked in concentration on a stick he repeatedly tossed into the air. A traveler who chanced upon the scene watched in curiosity as the shaman repeated the process over and over.

"What are you doing?" interrupted the traveler.

"I am asking the medicine stick which way I am to go," replied the witch doctor. "As it falls to the ground it points the way."

"And why do you throw it so many times?" the traveler asked.

"Because," admitted the shaman, "I don't want to go where the stick is pointing!"

Most of us want to be more submissive and less subjective than the witch doctor, yet an explicit definition of our calling eludes many of us. Some of us consider our own experience too intensely personal and subjective to reveal, much less recommend to others. Yet unless we are drawn to our place of ministry by a sense of God's leading, a paralyzing ambivalence will infect our motives. The call must be near the heart of ministerial motives.

Shepherd

The next metaphor—shepherd—speaks of relationships. In ancient Palestine a shepherd was not hired through a downtown employment office. The shepherding task demanded more than a hireling—someone so desperate for work he could be persuaded to camp in a pasture for pay. An authentic shepherd made the hills his permanent home. His life centered on his sheep. When lambs were born, the first hands to caress them were the shepherd's, and the first voice to greet their ears was the shepherd's voice. The growing lambs came to associate the resonance of that voice and the stroking of those hands with green pastures and still waters. By the time the lambs were fully grown, an intimate, trusting relationship was bonded between sheep and shepherd.

Something resembling this sheep-shepherd relationship is surely not too much to expect between a preacher and a church. God's servant enters a serious commitment when taking responsibility for feeding a congregation. So does the church. Minister and congregation will be trekking the hills together, crossing treacherous chasms, braving icy storms, and facing hungry wolves. Together they will also graze in green pastures and rest by still waters, where their relationships with each other and with God will flourish. Effective ministry comes from authentic relationships, and, as we have underscored repeatedly in these pages, such relationships take time.

Covenant

When a relationship is viewed as a covenant, its strength grows dramatically. Broken covenants result in broken hearts, whether in marriages or churches. When covenants are superficial, a minister may become more hireling than shepherd and a spouse more halfhearted roommate than lover. The church-preacher covenant should be considered a solemn agreement with God as its witness, and be honored as such.

Don't Move When . . .

Frequently, the urge to move strikes on blue Monday mornings, tempting us to move for all the wrong reasons. When is it seldom a good idea to move?

Frustration

First, do not move when *frustrated* that church growth has plateaued. Most churches experience periodic plateaus. A plateau may end in a drop off or form the footstool of a mountain—depending on your perspective! Using numbers as the lone criterion for effectiveness may need re-evaluation, as well.

Of course, our wart-ridden old congregation doesn't match our ideal. No church does. It's easy to forget that often the attractiveness of a prospective church exists only in the eye of the frustrated beholder. In my own case I am haunted by this question: If I have failed to lead this church into growth, what makes me think I will do it with another?

Problem Person

Second, *do not move simply because a problem person is making you miserable.* Most of us have endured those agonizing weeks when anywhere else looked appealing—anywhere to get away from that intolerable but unavoidable "someone" in the church.

In many such weeks I have reminded myself, "This impossible character could actually be an opportunity for personal growth. Be careful! You could be running from something God is trying to teach you. Besides, every church, even the next one, harbors at least one pain in the neck."

Money

Third, don't move just because *more money* is offered elsewhere. Remember the assumption underlying minister-church relationships: call, shepherd, and covenant? To answer a call only because it promises a generous boost in salary and prestige may not honor covenant or reflect the shepherd's heart. Upward mobility is no sin in itself, but the desire for well-situated positions is spiritually perilous. Seldom, if ever, is a larger salary to be taken in itself as a call of God.

Hurt

Fourth, when *I've been hurt* is not the time to consider a move. No one likes to hang around abusive people, and God does not require a vow of masochism. Pain, however, is not always symptomatic of a ministry gone wrong. More often, pain can be the very means God uses to accomplish necessary growth as well as fruitful ministry. I once believed it *possible* that a church might bring suffering to a minister. I now believe it is *inevitable*. There is no long-term, life-changing ministry without pain. We cannot confront evil and live with our fellow sin-victims without living at the edge of agony. I try to remember that God's most awesome deed was accomplished in his deepest suffering. Remember! We, also, are called to "share his suffering."

Of course, pain can also be self-inflicted. If I have been hurt too many times by too many people, I need to evaluate. Problems and disappointments can't always be someone else's fault.

Painful though it may be, reviewing the history of my own embattled relationships can be an ideal growth opportunity. During the early stages of my relationship with the Highland church, I wondered why such good people often became hostile with me, "a nice young man just trying to serve God." In the rearview mirror, I see a miracle that these people tolerated some of my attitudes.

The sense of calling, the shepherd relationship, and covenant all deepen and strengthen the minister-congregation bond as it grows over time. Sand lot football players roam the field and hog the ball but don't really help the team. The real pros stay home and play their positions. They help their teams become winners.

Dear preacher friend, at the moment it may seem like the way toward "success" in ministry is through mobility—to find the right church, to ride the wave, to play the ball. But if we keep moving away from the tough stuff toward the bright spots, eventually we ourselves will shrink as men—and the Kingdom will lose. But over the long haul, churches "win" through long tenure of ministry. And through long tenure, men of God keep growing. So hang in, for your own good, for the growth of the Kingdom, and for the glory of God. You will find freshness for the far journey.

18

A TIME TO GO

As surely as grievances real or imagined can seduce us to move for inappropriate reasons, healthy factors sometimes compel us to go. Leaving too soon can be tragic. But in some situations staying too long can be equally disastrous. Here are four scenarios that might call for a move:

Integrity

First, it may be time for a move when staying with the present church violates my integrity. For example, sometimes pulpit and pew honestly part company theologically. Other times the convictions of minister and members fall completely at odds over the direction a church should take. To remain in a church in violation of one's conscience breaks a higher covenant than the relationship between minister and congregation. One's sacred personal covenant with Almighty God obviously has first priority.

Family Needs

Second, a move might be the most godly option when family needs would be ignored by staying. Marriages have been damaged, emotional health impaired, even faith destroyed out of misguided loyalty to a ministry. Covenant commitment to family must take precedence over one's commitment to a church.

Some dear friends Joe and Carol confronted the crunch between ministerial possibilities and family needs. "I've found myself in the most fruitful ministry of my life. I feel I ought to stay. But Carol is miserable here," Joe confessed. "She has always been outgoing and had loads of friends wherever we have been. Somehow, she just can't connect here at Oakhaven. She's given it a good shot, over two years, but things are not getting any better. Is Satan luring me away from a good work through my own wife? Or is Carol my first priority?"

Joe decided to move. After more than two years, God is blessing Joe's ministry at Hope Valley far beyond what Joe could have imagined at Oakhaven. Even better news: Carol is blossoming again. She enjoys a sense of belonging, and God is using her tremendously.

Did Joe and Carol make a good decision? Didn't Jesus say, "If you love family more than me, you are not worthy of me?" My response is that commitment to Jesus must not be confused with our obligations to a given congregation. God made families long before He made churches.

Minister-Congregation Relationship

Third, when the relationship between minister and congregation no longer exists, a move is in order. In a marriage, when trust has been destroyed through infidelity, or when one partner no longer wants anything to do with the other, some would contend the relationship has already, in a sense, ended.

When are things over between minister and a church? Who knows for sure? But is there any point in staying when my credibility has been irreparably damaged? When the church no longer wants me, for whatever reasons, a relationship no longer exists. Conversely, when leaders of a church have consistently betrayed me, my trust in them will be shattered. When either of these conditions exists, covenant has been broken, and I am, in fact, no longer a shepherd of that flock.

God's Will

Fourth, a move is definitely right when it is clearly the will of God that I go to a specific new ministry. While our first three scenarios indicate a move for somewhat negative reasons, this fourth one is a positive indicator—being Spirit-led to new fields, rather than being driven from an old one.

How can I determine whether I am being driven or led? I must gather the hard information indispensable to sound planning. I need a no-nonsense understanding of the prospective church.

But even after the spadework has been done, I also need some certainty that God is beckoning in a new direction.

Discerning the will of God is not always simple. Sometimes in our intent to search for God's guidance, we wind up inside a subjective and confusing house of mirrors. Passion for divine guidance must be tempered by godly caution.

Discernment begins on our knees; thus, a healthy decision is bathed in prayer from beginning to end. We know that God also reveals His purposes through Scripture, so people of prayer will turn also to the Word.

But eventually, the seeker must confront specifics not addressed in Scripture, and God often leads through the counsel of wise and godly people. In the final analysis, crossroads decisions are usually very lonely. But the journey to the point of decision is best traveled in the company of several trusted confidants.

The Lord may also lead through convicting circumstances, troubled conscience, and my own spiritual gifts. I must resist the deadly inclination to silence my nagging questions:

Toward what are the events of life pointing me?

- Could God be shaping me into an instrument better suited to another setting?
- Why do special kinds of people and needs in other places chronically tug at my conscience?
- What about my gifts?

- Am I neglecting my gifts in the demands of the present church?
- And what of my dreams?

At times the Lord may back us into a decision. My friend Jay learned this. "Jay," I probed, "Why did you move to Hope Rock?"

After a reflective moment, Jay responded, "When the call came from Hope Rock, everything looked right, but I sat down and generated a list of seventeen reasons why I shouldn't go. One by one, all those reasons evaporated. I knew it was God at work. When the reasons were all gone, I knew I had to move."

To attempt an exhaustive analysis of the ways and means God leads, however, would border on sacrilege. Who understands God's mysterious leading? Many factors, I am sure, are involved in the guidance process, yet any one of them taken by itself could be disastrously misleading. Yet all the available components, taken together, can produce a helpful grid for the minister desiring both freshness and the will of God.

Places of the Heart

Randy, my friend mentioned at the beginning of this chapter, stayed where he was for several more productive years, declining numerous calls from large churches offering higher salaries and more prestige. Joe, also mentioned earlier, moved in response to a call that had all the perks involved in Randy's offers. Their decisions left both at peace with God and immersed in richly anointed ministries. Each listened to counsel from the secret places of his heart. So must all of us.

In the final analysis, I must examine the purity of my own heart. God's will can never be clear to me if my desire to obey Him is not genuine. Jesus probes this nerve when He says, "If the light within you is darkness, how great is that darkness!" (Matt. 6:23b).

T. S. Eliot wrote, "The last temptation is the greatest treason: To do the right deed for the wrong reason."[1] Our reasons must be right, and any attempt to know God's leading will be futile if my heart is not genuine. But if my heart rests in God, I can be at the center of His will in any number of churches. Where I go and how long I stay are really beside the point.

The secret places of our hearts cannot be entered hurriedly. Silencing internal noises long enough to hear the still, small voice is not for the impatient. But across the ages those who have listened declare the results worthwhile. As M. L. Haskins wrote,

> I said to the man who stood
> at the gate of the year;
> "Give me a light
> that I may tread safely
> into the unknown!"
> And he replied:
> "Go out into the darkness and put your hand
> into the hand of God.
> That shall be to you
> better than light
> and safer than a known way."[2]

Endnotes for Section ❺

1. T. S. Eliot, Murder in the Cathedral (New York: Harcourt, Brace & World, Inc., 1935), 44.

2. M. Louise Haskins, "The Gate of the Year," in The Treasury of Religious Verse, ed. Donald T. Kauffman (Westwood, N. J.: Fleming H. Revell, Co., 1947), 99

EPILOGUE

"Bloody, but Unbowed . . ."

John Killinger tells of a British monarch who wriggled on his pew as some inept preacher "fulminated in the pulpit." When the royal figure could bear no more, he blurted an interruption, "For God's sake man. Make sense, or come down!"[1] The king had far greater respect for the pulpit than did the preacher.

Preaching still counts today. The crisis of trust has not erased the central need and hunger for the preaching of the Word. Yet we preachers are often tempted to lose sight of this need, to underestimate the importance of our calling.

Maybe you found yourself at your twenty year class reunion, amazed at how your old buddies have succeeded. Some are now attorneys, investment bankers, surgeons, professors, CEO's, and senators. So you stood with your back to the punch bowl, trying to look important (or invisible), as they gushed success stories. But inside you battled a sinking feeling. Self-doubt had you wondering, "Have I let the action pass me by? The real difference seems to be made in the boardrooms, the marketplace, the courts, and the state house. And what have I got to show for my efforts?"

You weren't helped any by the comments either. One old friend from the past, spotting you near the fringe of the circle boomed, "Oh, hi, Lynn. How are things down at the church? Do you think you'll ever leave Muleshoe? But then, guess

it's a nice secure job. Work one hour on Sunday.
Ha! Ha! Say, maybe I've been called to preach. I
love fried chicken and I hate work. Ha! Ha! Hey
did you guys see that sign in the men's room over
the hot-air hand dryer? Says, 'push this button
and get a thirty-second message from Lynn Anderson.'"

"Did you hear the one about the preacher .. ?"

But don't let appearances demoralize you or
the jokes mislead you. My friend Roy Osborne
helped me when he explained that preacher jokes
are often actually a left-handed way people affirm
our importance. Have you noticed that jokes seem
funniest when they are about awesome things
like death, sex, parent-child relationships (witness Bill Cosby), and religion? Humor is usually
about issues so big they make us uncomfortable,
and we must laugh to ease our awkwardness.

I believe Roy is right. When people tell
preacher jokes, even though they don't always
realize it, they may be saying, "I don't understand
much of what you are about, but what you are
doing is profoundly important to me."

Something else I have noticed over the far
journey; in spite of the crisis of trust, many of my
old buddies in their power suits and European
automobiles with mobile fax-phones keep showing
up in front of my pulpit. I think they are hoping
for a word from God! They often take me far more
seriously than I dare to take myself.

During the writing of his doctoral thesis, Tom
Sibley polled preachers, elders, and "people in the
pew" on their views concerning the relative importance of preaching within the total task of the
minister.[2] To Sibley's surprise, of the three groups,

the people in the pew attached the greatest importance to preaching. In fact, they clearly saw preaching as the single most important task of the minister. Interestingly enough, elders considered preaching significantly less important than did the congregations. And, bingo, you guessed it, of all three groups, the preachers themselves gave preaching the lowest relative importance rating!

Sibley's findings confirm my suspicions. The preachers who value preaching the most are the ones who do it well. The ones who place minimal value on the pulpit tend to put little energy into their sermon preparation; thus, they preach poorly. Resulting negative feedback further confirms the preacher's low estimate of the value of preaching. Consequently, the law of diminishing returns rules his pulpit. On the other hand, the positive feedback from good preaching encourages even better preaching, so that the preacher's confidence in preaching grows, producing an upward spiral of freshness, vitality, and usefulness in the Kingdom.

After thirty-five years of preaching, I now believe in the power of the pulpit more than ever, and I invest far more into it than ever in my life. Feelings of futility have long since been all but permanently banished by the facts in my BD File. Over the far journey, this file has grown to be several feet thick, bulging with letters I have received from real live folks chronicling pivotal differences made by specific sermons—makes terrific reading on a "bad day."

We were not given a heavenly thesaurus, so we must use our own weak and partial human words to speak about the Father. "Pity the poor preacher who has to stand in a pulpit talking to men about God. See the little man with a yardstick trying to measure the horizons."[3] Our words, at our best, are sorry, inadequate pointers toward heaven. Yet, words are all we have to convey the yearnings and hopes of our souls.

We are clay pots, but we are not crack-pots. We are in His hands, and our flimsy words alter eternal realities. When a clay pot who is spirit-filled, Scripture-saturated, prayer-armed, servant-hearted, God-adoring, and Christ-following speaks the word of God, things happen, whether the preacher is aware of it or not. God smiles, angels applaud, hell quakes, and lives change.

So, preach on, *passionately*, in season and out. Heaven will keep you fresh for the far journey.

Endnotes for Epilogue

1. John Killinger, *The Centrality of Preaching in the Total Task of Ministry* (Dallas: Word Publishing, 1969), 3.

2. Tom Sibley, *Competency-Based Ministry Education and Training Program Development by a Consortium of Churches, Organizations, and Educators, Doctor of Ministry Product Thesis,* Wester Conservative Baptist Theological Seminary, Portland, Oregon, 1984.

3. J. Wallace Hamilton, *Who Goes There?* (Westwood, N. J.: Fleming H. Revell Company, 1968), 14.

Notes